MW00618883

Dear Sandy

Copyright © 2015 by the Author,
Jennifer Sweete

Dear Sandy is self-published by the author.

Dear Sandy

The letter that wrote itself into a Book

FIRST EDITION

This book is dedicated to
all of my teachers in life,
great and small, alike.

Dear Sandy

CONTENTS

Note to self:

"The beginning is the most important
part of the work."

- Plato

Preface

TO THE READER: This book began as a letter to a friend whom I cherish. It is a letter about gratitude, love, and transformation. With her and my express written permission to accept the forfeiting of our anonymity in any self-actualizing program that we may be a part of, it is now a published work of love available for all to read and enjoy.

We are all "Sandy" and we all deserve the kind of Hope that grows into Faith when fed by Love, the kind of Love that shines its Light for any person who has a burning desire to Hope for nothing less than a miracle of healing.

I would be remiss to write what you are about to read without first stating that within this letter all references to any wellness programs mentioned within, are in no way meant to represent the founders or the programs in any manner other than from my own personal experience and point of view. Though not intended to be promotional material for any singular wellness program, we offer this letter as correlative material to all, providing additional perspective for those who wish to add self-discovery to their self-recovery and vice versa.

Due to the extraordinary accessibility of information during my lifetime, I am unable to reference here all of the many teachers of physics, psychology, and human health from whom I have gleaned much knowledge and healing of my spirit, mind, heart, and body over the decades. Yeshua ben Yosef, Carl Jung, George Ivanovich Gurdjieff, Amit Goswami, Thich Nhat Hanh, Ram Dass, John Fuchs, "Mother" Mirra Alfassa, the Dalai Lama, William Griffith Wilson and Dr. Robert H. Smith, are but to name a few. To list them all in this letter would increase its volume to the size of an encyclopedia.

Many proven programs and methods for healing our Whole Selves are put forth in this letter, including reference to the Twelve Step program as this letter is to commemorate my dear friend, Sandy's, achievement as we stand together, hand in hand on the twelfth step today in celebration of our lives now well lived in the spirit of love.

If you, the reader, should determine that any part(s) of this letter seem misrepresentative or in conflict with what you believe to be true about the founders or content of any health and wellness programs or tools mentioned herein, please feel free to disregard those part(s) or feel free to toss the whole letter into your shredder. We must all honor where we are in our process in each moment.

I have learned, many times over, that I can only express my own personal experience and perspective, but can have no expectation of how someone else may perceive it. So, as we say in all true healing endeavors, "Take what you need and leave the rest."

My mission is simply to share a combo-platter of the knowledge and wisdom I have amassed with gratitude throughout the years as it pertains to elevating us to a higher state of being happy, healthy, and whole. To build a framework that can serve as a starting point and provide guidance for those in the process of rebuilding and renewing their lives.

In the beginning, we must learn to discern fantasy from fact. We must have more than a mere fleeting desire to change our inner and outer lives. The actualization of such a profound change must come from a united mind and we humans are rarely in possession of such. The work necessary to attain such a state of mind is hardly comparable to the comfort of a fluffy pillow. By necessity, there will be some kneading and pounding of the ego to get us into shape.

We'll need to open the doors of our minds

and let go of our old ways of thinking. Unhealthy thought patterns are like tightening tourniquets wound around our brains, separating us from the flow of life's eternal wisdom by creating the illusion that we are separate from our source. When we reach beyond our mundane existence to acknowledge forces of energy more powerful than our own, we are no longer subservient to ordinary ego limitations and thus can achieve extraordinary goals.

For the ego that believes it is All That Is, consider trying to turn on a light bulb with no electricity. The integrity of the bulb and its contents are vital but useless without a charge provided by an electrical force. Yet, even the perfect electrical current can't light up a burnt-out bulb without it first being repaired.

As much as we need to be "plugged in" to our own power source, our personal integrity is just as vital. How can we expect to bode well through the intense shocks of living and dying if we haven't developed the strength to withstand life's stormy moments? Developing strength of heart and mind requires no less of a workout than does developing strength in the physical body. If going to the gym for our morning workout is a drag, it's because we're not making it fun. When we add fun, it becomes something we look forward to. When we do the same for our inner work, we get the same positive results. It's really a matter of redefining our definition of *fun*.

There exist practical proven methods for circumventing ego, and reprogramming our inner and outer lives, that are quite exhilarating. Conscious Labor and Intentional Suffering are not equal to swinging a pick on a chain gang. We are not looking to trade our out-of-order lives for a life of equal misery, but we *are* looking to accept the fact that the results we are striving for are going to require intense efforts from us to bring them into being.

It's been the experience of many, including myself, that our largest efforts must be directed toward rigorous honesty, for without honesty we cannot dig to the deepest or reach to the highest levels required for authentic conscious change. To perceive and confront our own self-deceptive natures is our supreme aim. We learn to do this with compassion for ourselves and for others.

It's not unusual to want to share our newly born enlightenment with the world. Not everyone is ready, willing, or able to join in the celebration, however. One of the most riveting challenges facing us in our efforts to grow and expand our awareness of our selves and the world around us is our ability to detach with love from those who are still looking for an easier, softer way.

For those who *are* willing to participate in this more challenging, yet infinitely rewarding journey—a congratulatory welcome!

This intrinsically invaluable work on oneself seasons our souls and our very example becomes a gift for others who wish for similar healing.

As you read onward, know that I hold the Hope in Faith and Love that you who are dedicated to working along the path of spiritual self-discovery and recovery may find, here in this heartfelt letter to my esteemed friend, some nugget of golden truth that may be a gift to you en route toward a bright and beautiful present.

Note to self:

Surround yourself with people who are
working along spiritual lines and you will
always know someone you can trust
to guide you back to reality.

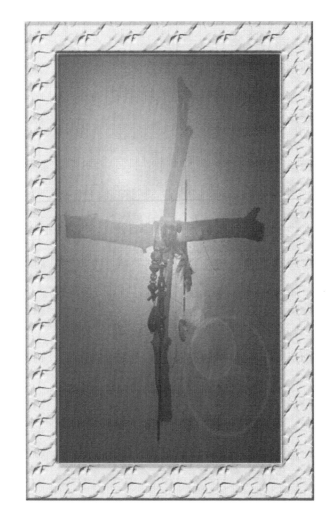

Dear Sandy,

Thank you for choosing me to sponsor you through your recovery from self-imploding. The wise teachings of many masters have helped to carve a clear path for millions of us to travel on our journey to reclaim rightful alignment of body, mind and spirit. I am but a messenger carrying the message of Hope to you. You are the only one who can take the Hope and crystallize it into Faith —not the blind faith of fools and charlatans, but the rock solid Faith of those who truly wish to know Divine Love and are willing to grow along spiritual lines.

As a new year approaches, I am reminded that gratitude for each breath of life, for each miracle no matter how great or small, for each lesson whether gentle or fierce, for each opportunity to turn to our Source for guidance and love opens the gate for yet more gifts to enter. In my gratitude for you in my life, I am inspired to share a deeper appreciation of this amazing healing process as I have come to understand it.

Humanity now has access to a wide variety of recovery programs, all of which seem to have sprung from ancient teachings adopted by many cultures across the globe. In this new millennium, there's a recovery program for nearly every addiction we can think of—from drugs and alcohol to sex, food, and video games. Whether we find ourselves addicted to mood-altering substances or to mood-altering personalities, or both, a recovery program can show us the way to a happier, healthier life.

Too often, however, we humans prefer to keep the focus on one particular addiction rather than address the addictive nature of the human condition at its root. Those with even the best intentions do not always address this root conditioning.

Keeping the focus on any particular brand of addictive madness tends to keep the focus on the actual thing that our focus should be rising far and above. I'd like to take this opportunity to peel away some of the layers of self-deception that ensnare too many and, instead, broaden our horizons to encompass a more powerful and unified healing that can set us free to reach our full potential and beyond.

More reveals itself when we blend the healing aspects of spiritual recovery programs with the wisdom of spiritual discovery bestowed upon us by many remarkable, awe-inspiring teachers that have traversed this life-on-planet-earth world through time immemorial.

In the context of this work on oneself, the word "spiritual" refers to no specific religious belief or system, but to wholeness within one's own self and a clear and present connection with a power greater than one's self.

Many common threads bind together the voluminous teachings of the wise souls who have endeavored to elevate the consciousness of humanity throughout numerous cultures and eras. My aim is to highlight and harmonize some of these teachings, that you might find it useful to have such a reference guide in your life, your continued healing, and your ever-present spiritual awakening.

I offer nothing new here, as all that I can share is what has existed since the beginning of All and Everything—Truth. I share here my own experience from my own perspective, and the results of my repeated verification of this truth. This is my gift to you that I give humbly and unconditionally, not only through these words, but also by being the living example of all of which I speak.

Thank you for being my inspiration to write.

Note to self:

The first person
to take your advice
should be you.

Amazing Grace

It's like money in the bank. It's the cement truck crawling up the highway in front of you—the one you can't get around—that keeps you from being in the three car accident you eventually pass by with a shudder to think that it might have been you. It's the police person giving you a warning instead of a ticket. It's the gentleman in the parking lot catching your ten dollar bill as the wind tries to snatch it from you while loading groceries into your car. It's the lady in the library giving you a free pass on your late fee. It's the person and/or program that shows up in your life just when you need them most. It's Lady Luck. It's Providence. It's Grace pure and simple, an investment worth nurturing.

Where does it come from? How do you know you have it? How do you make more of it? How do you know when you're spending it? How do you know what your budget is so you don't go bankrupt? Guess how many jellybeans are in the jar.

You've probably already surmised there's some quantum physics involved here, but we're not going to go into all that because the aim is to keep it simple. If you're the jar and the jellybeans represent the amount of energy contained within you then it stands to reason that a full jar is a power-packed goal. Most of us are short a few jellybeans. Since we're eating them to stay alive and trading them for other goodies on a daily basis, we need to figure out how to get new jellybeans every day. We really only have two options—we can get them from someone else by hook or by crook, or we can learn how to make our own. The former is catch-as-catch-can, whereas the latter is fairly fool-proof.

When making jellybeans, one needs certain ingredients. All matter consists of various molecules. All molecules consist of various atoms. All atoms consist of various subatomic particles. Etcetera. How do you like your jellybeans? Coarse? Fine? Sweet? Tart? Soft? Chewy? Tacky? What is the flavor of Grace? Grab your apron and let's do some baking so we can get a taste.

Where does Grace come from? Energy— one that is far more refined than the stuff we use to play basketball or go for our morning jog. How do you know you have some? Pay attention. Most of us only know we have it when we're spending it, and that's usually after the fact, if at all. How can you create a budget for Grace when you don't know how much you have or when and where you're going to spend it—or lose it—and you don't know how to make more?

When we're present, Grace fills us. When we make efforts to be present, Grace fills us. When we meditate, Grace fills us. When we make efforts to meditate, Grace fills us. When we let go of the ego's attachment to people, places, things, and outcomes, Grace fills us. When we make efforts to let go of the ego's attachment to people, places, things, and outcomes, Grace fills us. When we choose Faith over fear, Grace fills us. When we make efforts to choose Faith over fear, Grace fills us. When we're on autopilot, however, we're susceptible to falling from Grace in a million different ways—jellybeans spilling all over the place.

By the Grace of something greater than you or me, we are here, now, about to share in the making of a better world because a better you and me makes the whole world a better place for all of us. You can take that to the bank.

Fallen Angels

$\mathcal{A}$ is interesting to read the analogous stories from divergent cultures describing the fall of heaven's angels to this earthly domain. For what purpose in a world of duality would anyone or anything fall from Grace if not to have the opportunity to rise again by Grace?

The God of the Bible is said to have been born in the flesh of Yeshua (aka Jesus) to die from the flesh and rise again in the Spirit. Many cultures share similar stories, all of which at the very least symbolize the cyclical nature of our universe.

Simple physics demonstrates that what goes up must come down and vice versa. Like the trusty sword, all must find its balancing point in a world of dual expression. The concept of Karma is simply the necessity of balance in a universe made eternal by the infinitely reassuring, revitalizing system of reciprocal maintenance in which we play our part.

Sometimes our part is painful and we

wonder why humans must suffer so greatly in life. There is a saying that pain is inevitable yet suffering is optional. Painful experiences and personal life-challenges have the capacity to transform into something positive when the lessons learned from these experiences are passed along to others. When we receive the gift of a new perspective on life, there is much reward in paying it forward.

Each trial, once experienced and over-come, becomes knowledge fused into one's being. That knowledge is then available for the person(s) who inevitably appears in one's life at precisely the time he-she-they are entering such a trial in their own lives. Coincidence? If you believe in such a thing as coincidence, you might want to keep reading as you may be inclined to think about it quite differently in the process of self-discovery ahead.

Like many of us, there was a period in my life when I fell from Grace. It didn't happen in a moment, an hour, or even a day, but my out of balance ego eventually permeated my flesh and bones, and twisted thinking took my life down some pretty slippery slopes. At each crossroads where salvation offered a release from such madness, I chose the path of least resistance that, predictably and consistently, led me to yet more insanity.

Such is the state of much of humanity. We opt for the path of least resistance because recovery is hard work and we simply don't want to *work that hard.* The irony is that the harder we work at not having to work that hard, the harder we have to work at everything.

It's a rough and tumble ride for some of us and will continue to be unless and until we acquire a burning desire to change—a flame so hot that we begin to wish with every cell in our being to be cooled and washed clean. In that moment Grace arrives and we are once again, lifted into heaven's embrace.

For some that moment comes with the dying breath of the body. For others it comes with the dying hold of the ego. In either case, we are reborn in some respect. Many ancient texts tell us that Yeshua, Buddha, and other great teachers devoted their lives to this revelation for all of humanity. The great truth they shared is that we have Free Will to choose whether to be reborn in each moment of life or in death alone.

If our souls, or *consciousness* if you will, have fallen from the lightness of their heavenly bodies, or *abodes,* into the denseness of these earthly bodies, the human body could, therefore, be considered an avatar for consciousness.

These dense earthly bodies are in many respects mechanical in nature and, as in all things mechanical, programming is essential for the animation of life and has the capacity to determine the path of the avatar, depending on the programmer's will. As all programming is by design prone to repetitive action, our mechanical man left on autopilot is subject to being trapped by his/her all too easily formed patterns and habits. Even our sense of morality is programmed into us by the society into which we are born and live.

True Conscience, on the other hand, is a spiritual attribute not subject to mechanical programming. True Conscience is not programmed morality, but is of a more divine nature, very much alive, and is the bridge that connects us with our Higher Power.

True Conscience is accessible through prayer and meditation, though mechanical habits can thwart such an attempt. In such a case where force of habit prevents us from forging ahead, the application of certain shocks are necessary to interrupt ingrained patterns with enough veracity to allow the ray of divine light, referred to as the Sunlight of the Spirit, to activate True Conscience within us.

The process of freeing our will from mechanical patterning, activating True Conscience within us, and communing with our Higher Power, is vital yet seldom taught or talked about in ordinary everyday life. Nor is it something another can do for us. It is an alchemical process, and it is an *inside job*.

There are a few present-day schools that teach this internal chemical process, albeit many remain shadowed from the public eye. Fortunately, the Twelve Step program is one particular source of education toward spiritual awakening that serves in the public domain to teach this process in its most basic format that anyone may taste this salvation offered to all who wish to *work that hard*.

We, who have fallen from Grace, must come to understand that from which we have parted, and exert great efforts to rise again. However, the question remains, must we hit the bottom of the ego's barrel with the hope we will bounce, giving us our only momentum for flight? What happens to the fragile ones who hit the bottom? Like a raw egg, it can be a messy outcome. For those who have worked toward developing more flexibility and strength, bouncing is more likely to occur, but *oh the pain* for those more apt to crack on the pavement below.

There is another possibility to consider—

the possibility that one might intentionally raise the so-called bottom that even the fragile may not break, and fragile and strong alike might initiate their own momentum without need of a great deal of bounce, if any at all. For this to be a viable alternative, the creation of one's own burning desire to evolve spiritually must become a matter of *conscious choice* rather than *formidable fate*.

By taking personal responsibility for our own spiritual growth, engaging educated and reliable people to hold us accountable for our actions toward our goals, humbling our egomania, and strengthening our connection with a power greater than ourselves in order to reach the Sunlight of the Spirit, we may triumph.

Through honesty, humility, focus, prayer and meditation we, like fallen angels who have been remolded by the hands of Grace, may rise.

Stairway Toward Heaven

*W*hatever method or program we use to pull ourselves up from however far we have fallen and by whatever means, we will have to take it one step at a time. I have found it apparent that the founders of the Twelve Step program originally outlined their path to recovery with great thought and understanding and, evidently, a burning desire that brought divine intervention into their lives and since then, to millions of others.

My personal synopsis of the twelve steps toward recovery goes something like this:

1. Introduction to Alchemy = Admitting that self-reliance is not enough. In a world of Duality the only way to gain anything is to first let go of it. Neutralizing Resisting Force by dropping our end of the rope eliminates struggle and invites the true power of Grace into our lives. ***Honesty and Humility required.**

2. Believing in Hope = Switching from "Seeing is Believing" to "Believing is Seeing" is the straightest route to sanity for those of us who have seen too much darkness and believed in too little light. ***Honesty and Humility required.**

3. Faith in the Unknowable = A closed mind is a dark room. Faith is a flashlight that shows us the door. ***Honesty and Humility required.**

4. "Know Thyself" = Self-discovery is like digging for buried treasure in a bone yard. You get to the treasure only after sorting through the debris. A clean closet should contain no skeletons from the past (unless you happen to be an anthropologist, chiropractor, or store your Halloween decorations there). Justifying and rationalizing are out of the question. As a wise person once told me, when taking self-inventory it's important to keep in mind that rationalizing is the equivalent of mental masturbation—all you're doing is screwing yourself. ***Honesty and Humility required.**

5. Admission of Imperfection = We *cannot* fix it until we have established with certainty that it is broken. ***Honesty and Humility required.**

6. Readiness for Repair = We *will not* fix it until we

have confirmed that it can assuredly be repaired. Recognizing that we need the assistance of someone who has the knowledge and experience necessary for this repair job is essential to the continuation of this healing process. ***Honesty and Humility required.**

7. Assistance with Repair = Making the call to the Higher Power repair and maintenance company for assistance. I view this effort to contact a power greater than myself as though I am dialing across dimensions. ***Honesty and Humility required.**

8. Repairing the Ego = Making an in-depth amends TO-DO list is a humbling experience for the ego. ***Honesty and Humility required.**

9. Repairing the Spirit = Making active and actual amends to those we have been less than kind to in the past (including ourselves) releases us to become whole with our souls again. In effect, we are grabbing the symbolic broom and dustpan and cleaning up our side of the street. ***Honesty and Humility required.**

10. Staying the Course = Repeat numbers 1 thru 9 daily – hourly, even. ***Honesty and Humility required.**

11. Alignment in an Awakened State of Being = Keeping in constant contact with the Higher Power repair and maintenance company not only keeps us alert, but also awakens us to higher states of being. In these higher states, we are open to the miraculous. ***Honesty and Humility required.**

12. Paying it Forward = Creates and strengthens accountability from all directions. ***Honesty and Humility required.**

I have always said that the first eleven steps helped me *lift* my fallen butt up off the floor and the twelfth step helps me *keep* my butt off the floor. In fact, the twelfth step does much more than that.

Remember that what goes up must also come down. Once at the top, we risk falling again unless we reach out, extending a hand in Grace to yet another who may climb. Each time we reach out a hand and help another person climb this stairway, we rise higher and higher. It is only by choosing this conscientious way that we might succeed in attaining new heights.

Thank you, Sandy, for climbing with me, for as you make each effort to reach the next step we are both strengthened in being and in resolve. As you have made yourself accountable to me, I too have made myself accountable to you.

When we extend our invitation to others by reaching out a welcoming hand, we embrace all that Yeshua taught us. We are as much redeemed as the amount of redemption we offer to others. Though not all are ready or willing to grasp our outstretched hand, we remain as fishers of men and women, quiet and patient and present for those who, in their burning desire to be saved from drowning in their own craziness, may grasp what we offer and begin the climb to safety and sanity.

What can these first eleven steps do for us that no other process can, lest it be the same but by another name? They can walk us through the incineration of our negative emotions—doubt, guilt, fear, and loneliness, to name but a few. They stand with us in the furnace of transformation and give us the promise of freedom within and without. They give us the kind of Hope that can be molded into Faith. They return to us the Love we had long since rejected and abandoned. They strip away the lies to reveal the truth and heal the wounds we have suffered upon the cross of our own making.

Many who have suffered in their lives could call themselves victims and protest that the cross they bear is of another's making. Perhaps a person was abused as a small child. How could one possibly be held responsible for such an experience? But, do we know all things? Do we really know where we have come from, who we may have been or what we may have done before coming to this life, or that our cross is even our own? Is the blame game useful to our evolution or simply an excuse for not wanting to *work that hard?*

Did Yeshua suffer on the cross for Himself or for all of humankind? Was He born consciously aware of His purpose in the universe or did He grow to learn how to choose His particular path in the glory of all Grace? How does this apply to the rest of us? Were we born knowing all things or are we meant to discover our own paths along the way?

Are we truly victims or could it be that by falling into physical form we are asleep and in need of awakening? Weakened, and in need of strengthening by the tests and challenges particular to our personal growth in order to rise again to our angelic state of being?

Perhaps this riddle of *victim or volunteer* will never be solved, but all true spiritual teachings offer us the certainty that regardless of the past, the present is the only time in which we can create a new and fruitful future.

We can finally let go of feeling responsible for holding the world on our shoulders. We can rid ourselves of the negative emotions that have hardened like rocks in our heads and hearts. We can grasp the concept of a power greater than ourselves, whether it be Gravity, Magnetism, the Group Conscience, or the God of our understanding. Provided we are willing to move our old manner of thinking out of the way, there is the chance that more truth will be revealed.

Applying the methods outlined in these programs, we can rid ourselves of a preposterous past, and mend all rifts behind us. We can stop the blame game, shed the guilt, and stamp out the shame. We can scratch out every judgment that we have ever pronounced as righteous upon people, places, and things, including ourselves, to a point where we cease to judge altogether.

We can be free of the heaviness of our cumbersome egos for without judgment there is no need for forgiveness and all is forgiven. We can peel away years of worry, sorrow, anger, and resentment. We can be free to love and be loved —a true spiritual awakening.

We do this by becoming honest, open, and willing to be held accountable for our actions. By strengthening our own spiritual core in this way, we can then offer our newfound stability to others. We first lean upon someone who is a solid pillar of accountability, and then we become the solid pillar of accountability for another to lean on us.

Upon the stairway toward heaven, we steady our gait. When we reach the "twelfth step" we pay it forward by offering our experience, strength, and hope to those who wish to follow on this path. Consequently, we rise toward Heaven by the very Grace from which we had fallen.

You are an angel, Sandy. You can choose to fly. This is your right.

Lest We Come Again as Little Children

$\mathscr{A}$ is often said that when we are born we are pure of heart and mind. Where, then, does heredity come into play? Science tells us that we inherit many allergies and diseases from our forebears. What of the old adage that the sins of the father will be visited upon the sons? Why do we travel the paths that we do?

There is actually much to consider when asking "why?" There are always a minimum of seven levels of reasoning for all things imagined, said, or done, with only two or three of them being transparent to the ordinary human mind and four or more to the extraordinary human mind.

If you were to ask most people if they truly wanted to know all the reasons why certain things happen in their lives, they would probably say "no thanks" or cherry pick only the reasons suitable to them. Nor does being the complex creatures that we are, and living the busy lives we choose to live, always allow for the kind of time necessary to dissect each and every reason for each and every occurrence in life.

There are monasteries full of monks who spend their lives contemplating such matters. We who live in the chaotic world of civilization, however, might find ourselves befuddled should we undertake such a mission as to query the multifaceted "why" of all occasions.

Knowing what we already know, if we wish to understand more fully, we ought to begin at the beginning—the law of *cause and effect.*

The first answer to "why" in any question pertains to the physicality of the occurrence. For example, "Why does Johnny repeatedly fall down the stairs?" Perhaps Johnny trips on his untied shoelaces, which causes him to take a tumble. Most people would be satisfied with this as the final word on the cause and effect for the situation. However, there is, by rule of nature, a second level of awareness and understanding to consider—the emotional cause.

What is Johnny feeling emotionally when he ignores his untied laces and sends himself sailing down the stairs arse over elbows? Might it be a negative emotion? Perhaps he is entertaining feelings of jealousy about the new boy in town in whom his girlfriend has taken a keen interest. Or, perhaps he is feeling betrayed at being demoted from captain on his high school football team or manager at his job. These negative emotions of jealousy or betrayal blind us with the sleep of a mind busied with thoughts other than on where we are and what we are doing.

This leads us to a third level of understanding—the "why" of his tumble in relation to his mental state. Perhaps his thoughts are on his feelings rather than focusing on the task-at-hand, which in this case should be but isn't, paying attention to walking down the stairs.

In effect, Johnny's mind, emotions, and body are no longer synchronized. Lack of this synchronization will inevitably lead him to these and other kinds of problems.

The key to the gates of heaven is within our reach when we recognize that our minds wander relentlessly when untethered. Our tendency to focus on the past, the future, or how we are feeling—emotionally or physically—rather than on the present moment, seems to be a universal dilemma.

Although it may appear that this lack of paying attention causes accidents to happen; in reality the chaos and disasters that befall us from not paying attention to the present moment's task-at-hand are *predictable* results. The fact that we continue to survive at all in this state of mental distraction seems more the *accident*.

In some ways, we do ascertain bits and pieces of this insight on a regular basis, at least in a general way. We will say to ourselves, "I simply wasn't paying attention to what I was doing." Unfortunately, we will move on to the next situation without giving much thought as to how to better master our attention because mastery of attention requires that we *work that hard*.

This brings us to the fourth level of understanding—seeing that there is a genuine need for work on mastery of attention. On this level a new type of *seeing* is happening, however our tendency is to blink once, then twice, forgetting about what we were in the process of seeing each time we remove our attention even for a moment. Often we forget not only *what* we have seen but even *that* we have seen.

This fourth level of understanding offers us the opportunity to begin our descent toward the root of the matter. If we can grasp this new awareness and remember the lesson long enough, we can move to the fifth level of understanding in which we can get a glimpse of what we can actually *do* about it.

What is this "something" we can do?

Inspired by an event such as this to see an underlying condition (4th level of understanding), we can begin to practice consistent self-observation (5th level of understanding). We can continue to attempt to recognize this underlying condition at play in our lives. If Johnny could see that his mind wanders, continually making him accident prone, and then consistently observe this conditioning at play in his life, he might actually create the possibility for change.

Sadly, few are willing to exert exceptional efforts to change their internal and, as a result, external conditions. Consequently, we have too few fallen angels who rise to the entirety of heights open to them. Yet, for those who do work that hard, there is more work, such as the sixth level of understanding—awareness of our root conditioning, and the seventh level, which can lead to the development of real objective Will and real permanent change.

We can practice understanding "why" on these levels and even ingrain the method as habit in our very beings. With enough practice, it can become a natural process for us. Beware, however, that to do this out of habit will mechanize the process. Once the process becomes mechanical, all is lost once again. Ah, yes, a conundrum, indeed, but one we relish as more friction for our inner fusion.

Being present is essential to the art of living consciously. As my Uncle Leftover used to say, "Keep your mind where your body is and everything will be alright."

To simplify, we can list the seven levels of "why" Johnny repeatedly falls down the stairs along with his cause-effect solutions here:

1) Physical state:
PROBLEM—untied shoelaces;
SOLUTION—tie your shoes, Johnny.

2) Emotional state:
PROBLEM—negative emotions;
SOLUTION—dissolve each negative emotion, Johnny.

3) Mental state:
PROBLEM—wandering thoughts;
SOLUTION—keep your mind where your body is and focus on the task-at-hand, Johnny.

4) Alignment state:
PROBLEM—physical, emotional, and mental states are misaligned, not being present, being asleep at the wheel;
SOLUTION—see your underlying condition of being unfocused and out of sync, Johnny.

5) Self-awareness state:

PROBLEM—attention is repeatedly not focused on the present moment;

SOLUTION—in everything you do, Johnny, constantly observe your underlying condition of being unfocused and out of sync.

6) Clarifying state:

PROBLEM—focusing one's attention on being present is too much work, don't want to *work that hard*;

SOLUTION—observe this root condition of "laziness" that is the underbelly (key feature) of your mechanical condition of inattentiveness, until you burn with desire to do whatever it takes to be mindful, present, and willing to work toward change, Johnny.

7) Pre-conscience state:

PROBLEM—time spent baking in a state of burning desire feels damned uncomfortable;

SOLUTION—get comfortable with being uncomfortable, Johnny, and use prayer and meditation to ask higher forces for assistance.

Johnny's friend Jane offers us another example. Jane struggles with health issues. She has been healthy one day and sick the next for years. One day Jane decided to ask why this pattern was in her life. Let's look at Jane's cause-effect relationship with her health.

1) Physical state:
PROBLEM—recurring illness;
SOLUTION—take better care of your health, Jane.

2) Emotional state:
PROBLEM—constant worry about a family member, worry stems from fear and fear is a negative emotion;
SOLUTION—dissolve each negative emotion, Jane.

3) Mental state:
PROBLEM—constantly thinking about ways to try to solve her family member's problems, wandering thoughts;
SOLUTION—keep your mind where your body is and focus on the task-at-hand, Jane.

4) Alignment state:
PROBLEM—physical, emotional, and mental states are misaligned, not being present, as if being asleep at the wheel, causing inatten-tiveness to self-care;

SOLUTION—see your underlying condition of being unfocused and out of sync, Jane.

5) Self-awareness state:
PROBLEM—attention is repeatedly not focused on the self-care task-at-hand;
SOLUTION—in every situation, constantly observe your underlying condition of being unfocused and out of sync, Jane.

6) Clarifying state:
PROBLEM—fear of not being able to control outcomes and environment defeats ability to focus attention on being present;
SOLUTION—observe this root condition of "fear of powerlessness" that is the underbelly (key feature) of your mechanical condition of inattentiveness, until you burn with desire to do whatever it takes to be mindful, present, and willing to work toward change, Jane.

7) Pre-conscience state:
PROBLEM—time spent baking in a state of burning desire feels damned uncomfortable;
SOLUTION—get comfortable with being uncomfortable, Jane, and use prayer and meditation to ask higher forces for assistance.

Jane might observe that her *fear-of-powerlessness* programming, stemming from a childhood wherein she was punished when people and things were not running smoothly, now requires her to punish herself as an adult whenever she cannot control the people or things around her. Armed with this new awareness and the realization that worrying about others distracts her from staying true to her self-care regimen, a burning desire to change can develop, a Higher Power will respond to her plea for assistance, and transformation will naturally follow.

Like an Octave of Intention, this Octave of Understanding allows us to see a more complete picture of the internal programming that's running the show. When we get to the deeper "why," we can begin to address the "how" to reprogram our root conditioning.

We can only attempt to bring our three levels of understanding—physical, emotional, and mental—into alignment after we've made sufficient efforts to recognize their fundamental workings. Following this recognition, even stronger efforts are required to harness these three parts of our living being together so they can be observed simultaneously going forward. As in the Serenity Prayer, we ask for the courage to change the things we *can*. This is where change truly begins.

The moment that we become sincerely grateful to enter into the pre-conscience state, and the burning desire for change becomes the heralding of conscious contact with a higher power, we have stepped upon the bridge of True Conscience.

As in the Serenity Prayer, we *accept* that our overall transformation is not something that we can accomplish by ourselves. For it is only through this acceptance that assistance from a force greater than our mortal selves becomes available to us in ways we may never have thought possible.

As the Serenity Prayer also suggests, it is imperative to acquire the wisdom to know whether we are at a place in our understanding that requires our efforts to wrestle with the tangled wires of our programming, or requires our efforts to "let go and let God."

Though the problems unveiled in each of these seven states will vary by individual and life circumstances, many of us will discover that we often share Johnny and Jane's underlying conditions of poor attention, fear of powerlessness, and laziness to do what is necessary to transform at our deepest levels of being. Because our external situations in life are a reflection of our internal conditioning, it's really no surprise that humanity's present state of affairs is in such disharmony.

When through this process we come to recognize that we know next to nothing about the depth and breadth of whom and what we truly are, we are at the beginning. We can see that we are quite clumsy in our bodies—physical, emotional, and mental—much like a little child.

From here, we can begin to climb toward a new understanding of what true Freedom, real Will, and authentic Spiritual Awakening actually mean. Change occurs only when we are willing to acknowledge that it is necessary.

Like a child learning to walk for the first time, we must humble our egos to address our challenges effectively, exerting maximal efforts to *work that hard.*

Principles Before Multiple Personalities

*W*hen working together, it's important to place the principles of a program of spiritual development above our conflicts of personality with other people in order to circumvent a plethora of unhealthy distractions. Much easier said than done, we must strive for progress rather than perfection.

All human beings are clothed with personalities assembled almost entirely of the mishmash of programming shoveled into our brains from people, places, things, and events that we may or may not have had any control over throughout our lives.

We are also genetically endowed with the programming our parents' DNA provided at the time of our conception, accompanied by whatever experiences we may have had before our birth. If it is true that conversations taking place outside of the womb are, somehow, heard by the human fetus during development (can you imagine what a playback of that recording must sound like?) there is no way we can know how these might possibly affect us later in life.

With all of these influences combined, what a mixed bag each of us brings to the table if we are being honest about it.

If you have ever attended a committee meeting of some type, you are probably well aware of how seldom people in attendance agree on everything. Imagine, then, how easy it would be to bribe or blackmail one or more leaders of any size or shape, business or politic, to bend in any direction. Temptation to concede for reward, especially after hours, days, weeks, or months of useless standoffs between irreconcilable person-alities, must be scintillating.

Now imagine the committee of thoughts in your own head. All those little voices carrying on about their wants and needs, likes and dislikes, and all of the contradictions that must collide and reconcile before any action can take place in your life. Who in there serves as the referee?

What happens when the essence of your ethics programming conflicts with your financial stability programming? What happens when your survival programming tells you that rejecting your spouse who cheated on or lied to you is the only way to protect yourself from further pain; while your morality programming tells you that for-giving your spouse is the only right thing to do to save your marriage and, depending on your religious upbringing, possibly your very soul? Yes, it is a tangled web within.

We call the cumulative tendencies toward a particular reaction or response from a person struggling with these perfectly normal internal contradictions on a daily basis, his/her *personality.* In groups, the real question becomes *which or whose principles shall we place above which or whose personalities?* The same question could apply to the space between our ears.

Psychiatry points to fragmented reactions or responses from our personalities and labels them *personality disorders.* They refer to these disorders as mental illness. If they are correct, then all of humanity is mentally ill with only degrees of separation.

What once used to be referred to by psychiatric professionals as a Split Personality became known as Multiple Personality Disorder and is now also known as Dissociative Identity Disorder. Perhaps the psychiatric professionals cannot make up their minds about what to call this fragmentation of personality for the very same reasons their patients are coming to see them. The outcome appears to be that neither doctor nor patient seems to be achieving maximal results of inner unity using conventional medical intervention.

There are more people being prescribed psychotropic drugs today than ever before. In my opinion, when numbing symptoms becomes preferential to addressing cause, something is systemically wrong with the whole process.

Since most people are rarely fully present, and most of those same people are unaware of whom and what they really are, their true purpose or potential, or how to begin to overcome life's many obstacles, then what pill can cure this ill?

Where, then, to turn for help when one realizes a problem of such magnitude exists? Of course, this again depends on how hard one is willing to work. When there is a burning desire for unity of body, mind, and spirit, then there is Hope; and where there is Hope there can be formed Faith, and solutions become available where there once seemed none.

Does a self-actualizing spiritual recovery program hold the answer for us? It may help, depending on underlying causes. Is medication necessary for some? Medication can in some cases, balance enough mental or chemical imbalances to begin and, in some cases, continue.

The healthiest and most fortunate results for the majority, however, are unlikely attainable under the influence of mind-altering substances, since the main mission is to seek and find that balance within one's natural self. "Physician, heal thyself," Yeshua said.

Of course, if a person has achieved his/her optimum physical, emotional, and mental health, and has reached an impasse toward any further gain, then diagnosis and treatment by a professional in the field of medicine is most certainly a consideration.

[NOTE: I am not a medical professional. What you read in this letter-book is not intended to override or replace the diagnosis and/or treatment plan of any medical professional. Please do not go off your meds without your physician's approval.]

The experiences of many on a path toward spiritual development indicate that when we relinquish control over all things, including our own insanity, to a Higher Power we have taken the first step toward healing. For, it is only in the letting go of control to a Higher Power that we gain any real control over our lives and attainment of our healing goals.

This requires a great deal of effort and is not for those who don't really want to *work that hard,* particularly because it must continue to be repeated again and again, minute by minute, day after day after day. Transformation of a life is a lifetime proposition. The rewards for such out-standng and humbling efforts are innumerable.

One day at a time, one minute at a time, one *seeing* at a time, is the principle that has the capacity to produce most of the natural chemical changes necessary to transform a fragmented personality into a unified one.

When viewed from this vantage point, the concept of placing healthy, spiritual principles before a multitude of personalities takes on a whole (pun intended) new meaning.

Humbly Yours

*F*or anyone who has suffered the pings and pangs of being humiliated, the very word "humility" can raise the hairs on a person's neck. Even more than their phonetic association, there can be a fine line between the two when a person's precious ego grows so fluffy and puffy there seems no room left for the rest of us to get through the doorway, thereby almost begging a somewhat deflating poke.

Ironically, fluffy, puffy people are often overcompensating for some lack of self-esteem, whether consciously or not.

Haven't most of us succumbed to this "best defense is a good offense" ego inflation at one time or another; perhaps even in the name of "righteousness"? Even the timid and shy person often entertains an air of righteousness quietly in his/her mind, as their sense of uniqueness, regardless of esteem, sequesters them from the crowd.

Having faced many trials in this human

form, one of my biggest struggles has been in the erring belief that I know best what is just and fair. Even to this day, I have to sit myself down and re-member that there is a Higher Power that knows better than I do.

The windowless walls of the ego's sub-jective perspective limit our point of view. When the only visible "why" is the mundane physical reasoning of our animal, instinct-based existence, how can we ever hope to see the bigger picture, let alone comprehend it.

Wallowing in the deep, dark well of un-reconciled past experiences, self-pity pours in like floodwaters, and helplessness and hopelessness become difficult to differentiate. As the t-shirt says, "Your mind is a dangerous neighborhood; never go there alone."

When self-reliance fails to produce a solution and we find ourselves trapped by the persistent illusion that we are alone and power-less, two options avail themselves to us. We can succumb to drowning in the ego's negativity, or we can let go of our limited beliefs and turn an open heart and mind toward a power beyond our understanding. When we choose to open to a Higher Power, an amazing thing happens—the peace of acceptance enters into our being like a rope lowered from above, and we are lifted once again into the Sunlight of the Spirit.

We come to realize, as we work toward wholeness of body, mind, and heart, that there are no victims in life, only volunteers.

Like the cycle of night and day, sleep and awakening, remembering and forgetting, the cycle of hope and despair is a part of life's natural rhythm. To find balance means that we cannot dwell in one or the other but, instead, we can learn to flow in nature's rhythm, and even learn to slow the swing of the drama-pendulum so that it no longer flings us so far and wide in either direction that we can barely hold on to our sanity. Breathe deeply and strive for humility.

It's far too easy to confuse humility with humiliation. Humiliation is a subjective group of mostly uncomfortable feelings and thoughts experienced by a person who, despite efforts to retreat, must face and recognize the message or lesson the humbling experience is providing. On a deeper level, there may be the recognition of one's inability to override, by mastery of will, the choice of the subconscious mind to attract the humiliating experience in the first place. Bearing in mind also that humiliating experiences can be messages that herald in true humbleness where a lack of humility has been festering. It places the responsibility for the necessity of the experience in our own laps, the very idea of which is quite humbling and clearly not always warmly received by many of us.

Most people will balk at the concept that we all magnetize to us every experience we get, good and bad alike, but that has more to do with the context in which the words "good" and "bad" are used.

When viewing all experiences as lessons to grow from, opportunities for change, fuel for energy, and friction for fusion, the terms "good" and "bad" must necessarily be replaced with "healthy" and "unhealthy" and/or "useful" and "not useful."

As spiritual beings having a human experience, we tend to judge our reality based on comfort, and comfort is measured subjectively. Before pooh-poohing this idea, take into consideration that one man's garbage is another man's treasure, just as one man's pain is another man's pleasure. It is all relative to the person having the experience.

We do not all share the same reactions to similar stimuli. The fakir has learned to tune out physical discomfort, and focus only on control of his/her body's reactions to pain and discomfort. The monk has learned to tune out the dramatic, and focus on only one emotion, their love of God.

The yogi has learned to tune out mental noise, focusing on only one mantra to obtain control of his/her mind.

To master one area is an enormous accomplishment, yet without bringing these three parts of our being into balance and harmony with one another and mastering their higher levels, leaves us wide open for humbling, possibly even humiliating, experiences in the areas that need bolstering.

How best then, to see the areas that need this strengthening? A good shock or poke maybe? Who is poking at you or pushing your buttons? Who is tripping your trigger? Who is bursting your bubble? And, *who* is asking "who?"

The better questions might be: *How can you disconnect that button? How can you disarm that trigger? Are you really happy living in that bubble anyway?* Can you trace today's painful, humiliating experience back to an earlier experience in your life, or another even earlier experience than that? How far back can you go before you perceive that, at the root, there is only the disturbance of your comfort zone and your expectation of yourself, others, and life? After all, what is an expectation but a pre-meditated resentment and verily a bubble waiting to be burst.

If bubbles are destined for bursting, then

would you prefer to be in charge of the process or leave the method and moment of your humbling to chance?

I am forever amazed at the inevitability of my humbling, and sometimes even amused at my Higher Power's sense of irony. I've also discovered that the daily humbling exercises I voluntarily perform to shrink my bubbles to a more manageable size help to avert the more painful humiliations that would surely befall me should lack of this oversight allow my bubbles to become the size of hot air balloons at the mercy of any ol' storm on the horizon.

Many spiritual development programs are designed to assist with this specific exercise, whether we ride into such a program huffing and puffing in an effort to keep our deflating balloons afloat or come crashing in with the tattered shreds of our high and mighty daredevil selves held tightly in our fists. Either way these programs have much to offer if and when, we are honest, open, and willing to receive the knowledge and put it to good use.

Listing our egos' grievances, checking in on how we helped create them in the first place, owning up to our *volunteering*, and admitting our shortcomings, initiates the cleaning up of our side of the street. To become truly accountable, we must become impeccably honest and forthright.

This process of developing greater humility frees us from the past in a more complete way than most, and dissolves many limitations that were once a major pain in the posterior.

There will still be times that only our Higher Power can give us the good poke, i.e.: shock, that might be required to shake us awake to see our inflated egos in action.

We can learn to appreciate these magical bubble-busting moments when we begin to see these enemies of our status quo as opportunities for growth rather than mere disruptors of our otherwise "bubbly" mood.

Garbage In, Garbage Out

It's trash day. Seven o'clock in the morning and you hear the sound of the crunching machine on wheels fast approaching. The sanitation engineers have arrived to carry away all the things you don't want to keep around.

Should be simple enough, but here is the trick—are you sure that you have gathered up all of the garbage that needs to go?

Have you emptied those trash baskets in the bathrooms? Have you picked up the piles of dead leaves from the yard? Have you bagged that successful mousetrap in the garage?

Have you removed all of the science projects from the refrigerator, at least the ones that are less likely to win you a Nobel Prize in the foreseen future?

Have you broken down those cardboard boxes? Have you separated out all the re-cyclables?

Are you certain you have gathered it all into one place for transport? Great! Garbage Out!

Remember to wave to the courageous people in the big, smelly truck, who are experts at hauling away your refuse. Be grateful for the right people for the right job.

Oops! Did you forget that the paper shredder is overflowing? How about that chicken carcass you tossed into a bag and stuck in the freezer to keep from spoiling until trash day? What about that putrid whatever-it-was-it-ain't-no-more there in the fuzzy plastic wrap, tucked behind the carrots at the bottom of the vegetable drawer in the fridge? You know—the one you missed in your hazy early morning haste? How could you have forgotten all these things?

We are the masters of forgetfulness. Like all rhythms in life, we cycle between forgetting and remembering. It is perfectly normal and nothing to be ashamed of, but it can be sooooo aggravating ... if we let it.

There is an old school of thought suggesting that evil can only enter through the door if we invite it in. Since the worst kind of evil is often the judgments that we foist upon ourselves it benefits us greatly to be not only aware of our surroundings, but also our in-dwellings—those thoughts and feelings we give permission to dwell within us.

Guilt and shame can be our undoing, so

spare yourself undue grief by giving yourself permission to flow with the rhythm of forgetting and remembering. As long as you are making efforts toward remembering, you will succeed at most everything you set out to accomplish.

Since being forgetful can be so annoying, we have three options. We can let it affect us negatively, we can laugh it off, or we can see it, observe it, and change it by changing the way we think and feel about it.

Quantum Physics has proven that only under observation is change the result.

Observation requires an observer. If we want to change something, we must first observe it. Self-observation yields inner change. Inner change yields outer change.

Begin with *attention*. Energy follows *attention*, not *intention*. You may have the best of intentions, but if you don't put your *attention* on your *intention* you'll end up drifting far from your aim.

This is the clearest demonstration of the hierarchy of *attention* and *intention* that I can think of: try driving down the road (preferably slowly on a wide, abandoned road since we don't want you to get injured or injure anyone else) and intend to go straight ahead. Now turn your eyes to the scenery out the passenger window to the right. You will quickly discover the car veering *unintentionally* to the right because it is following your *attention*, not your *intention*. Truly, the best intention you can have is to gain mastery over your attention.

So begin with *attention*. Energy follows attention. Form follows energy. Matter follows form. Consequently, the only things that truly *matter* are those we pay *attention* to, so attend to what matters most to you. Since we can only remember what we pay attention to, if what matters most to you just happens to be your intention to improve your attention, your memory will improve accordingly.

Beating yourself up about what you have forgotten is simply aiming all of your attention on forgetting rather than remembering. If you put your attention on remembering, then you will become a magnet for events that will help you see the obstacles in your way so you can dissolve them with the magic wand of self-observation and the magic potion of shifting your attention to the present moment.

The neat trick of self-observation is that by watching the ego's unhealthy behavior long enough, we simply get so deathly sick of it that the mere whiff of it approaching gives us the burning desire to consciously course-correct and head in a healthier direction.

Whether it's an emotional flair-up, a mental obsession, a physical craving, or any combination of these, the urge to escape present reality can be dissolved by consciousness if done before we act upon that urge. We must use our imaginations in the right way to follow everything through to its natural conclusion—look before leaping. This is where the work to master one's attention becomes crucial.

The very moment that we observe our "urge to surge" into unhealthy behavior, we can say to that part of ourselves, at whatever volume necessary, "Stop! Drop! And Breathe!"

After a deep breath, we can mentally project ourselves into the scene, whether we were yearning to lose ourselves in the saloon or the refrigerator, etc, or longing to chase down and try to control someone else's life choices instead of working on our own. How does it taste, sound, feel? What lighting, music, season, weather, or other circumstances are familiar? We can trace these associations back to identify what triggers the urge from the start.

We can also use our mind's eye to imagine forward that we eat the fridge empty, drink the bar dry, or shout a long lecture at someone whose behavior upsets us. On this imaginary journey we strive to remember that "morning after" feeling—the unsavory taste of regret, guilt, and shame that self-abandonment bestows upon us. Negative emotions we are well acquainted with. Repeating the same behavior and expecting different results? Insanity! Rather than more of the same, we have just taken the time to return to presence of mind.

We have come full circle to see that our sense of urgency to escape has now quieted, releasing its hold, and we can proceed further to be still and call on higher forces to assist with dissolving it completely and provide real direction in our lives.

Ta-da! Garbage out.

How did the garbage get in there to start with? Programming. Who did the programming? Everyone and everything that we have contact with in our lifetimes, programs us in one form or another.

There comes a day, however, when we can decide to become the programmer and, if we are willing to *work that hard*, we can actually become fairly good at it. There is one caveat, however. We can only do what we are prepared and have the knowledge to do, so we need to apprentice ourselves to someone who possesses both the knowledge and experience, someone who already knows how it's done.

In my experience, the most qualified teachers are those who consistently ask for direction from their Higher Power. Unfortunately, the folks who think they already know everything about bubble-busting reprogramming are living in a bubble.

Given the awareness that we all make bubbles and what happens to all bubbles, we might consider viewing all future uncomfortable experiences in our lives as our personalized bubble-busting, garbage-crunching teachers.

Given that our Higher Power is the ultimate knowledgeable and most experienced programmer of all, it makes sense that asking for direction through prayer and meditation is going to produce the most qualified guides and guidance for our Garbage Out endeavor.

Remember that the right person for the right job makes all the difference.

Putting the Fun in Dysfunctional

*N*obody said it would be easy, but nobody said it couldn't be fun! I have heard you cry with sorrow, Sandy, and I have heard you laugh with joy. Conversely, I have watched tears stream from your eyes in moments of revelation and celebration, and heard boisterous laughter erupt from your belly in the face of life, as you knew it, breaking to bits and pieces in a landslide of challenging events.

Tears of amazing joy and belly laughs at the absurdities in life are no stranger to those of us who have undertaken this work along spiritual lines. You are healthier than you know.

Those who cannot laugh at life are destined for misery, and those not moved to tears of jubilation at the miracles manifested by true contact with a Higher Power most certainly have a lot of shoveling to do to get to the depth of their heart of hearts.

To some, this might all sound backward, but isn't that the point? Reprogramming ourselves means doing things differently, thinking differently, and responding differently. For instance, many of us are programmed to *frown at the wrinkles on our faces*—do you see the irony in this?

I, personally, have learned never to trust anyone over thirty who has no laugh lines by their eyes. If the eyes are the windows to the soul, laugh lines let you know that the curtains are open. Learn to think differently and more truth will be revealed, hopefully bringing more than a few chuckles with it.

The greatest spiritual teachers agree that laughter is the best medicine. Laughing at our own foibles is most important!

Taking ourselves too seriously is usually the first part of our programming that needs to be reprogrammed. Yes, this is serious work as our lives depend on our dedication to it, but those who cannot learn to laugh at themselves are destined to drown in their despair.

Keep the fun in your dysfunction, and make sure to pass your infectious laugh and enthusiasm on to all who come to you with their own dysfunctional behavior, regardless of whether they come to stay or are simply passing through.

When we work along spiritual lines, we get healthier. Our bodies, though hardly invincible (as we have so aptly demonstrated in the reckless meanderings of our youth), if not damaged beyond repair, will begin to dance with determination.

As we bring our attention to what we eat and drink; to the balancing of our PH levels; to eliminating unnecessary chemicals from our bloodstreams, concentrating on absorbing the vitamins, minerals and nutrients that help our systems thrive; and to getting moderate exercise, sunshine, and fresh air, we begin to heal.

Our skin, teeth, nails, and hair are going to be nourished; our bones and muscles are going to strengthen; extra fat cells are going to dissolve; our brains will unscramble, and our eyes and smiles will brighten.

People who know us will inevitably notice, and many will comment positively. Strangers will smile at us, often wondering where our special glow is coming from. We will no longer fear the aging mirror in our bathrooms.

When we begin improving the health of the physical body, we set in place a firmer foundation for the mind and heart to follow. When the body is healthy, the mind and heart ease into serenity with less effort.

Meditating comes easier as the mind becomes clearer and more compliant to our wish for peace and quiet within. Our base emotions also become slower to fire up at the least provocation. Once these three characters—body, heart, and mind—are in alignment, our work along spiritual lines can accelerate in proportion.

To do this, of course, we must first come face to face with that force within us that resists change. There is no way to neutralize this resisting force if we are not even aware of its existence, so becoming aware of it is essential to our progress. This demands great effort to see this force in action and to discover the ways it compels us to fall from Grace as well as to acknowledge its importance in our rising upward into Grace.

We use meditation to strengthen our real Will for the successful fusion of the affirming and resisting forces. The ego's "little will" is useless in the face of resisting force as its programming will be conflicted and consequently can't be trusted to be thorough or consistent.

Pump it up! Meditation exercises allow us the opportunity to wrestle with resisting force. We pit conscious stillness against habitual movement, conscious movement against habitual stagnation, conscious silence against habitual inner talking, etc. The more often we do these exercises, the stronger Real Will can grow.

Another method we use to neutralize the resisting force is laughter. There is a reason the laughing Buddha is one of the most popular figures in history. He conceptualizes this truth in a simple persona for anyone who understands how thoroughly and completely the essence of laughter neutralizes unhealthy emotional and mental attachments, freeing us to be receptive to the rays of the Sunlight of the Spirit.

Whenever you feel the shadow of negativity creeping into your life, your work, your relationships, your heart and mind, Sandy, take a deep breath and laugh loudly at the absurdity of it all. It is only life. What goes down must come up, and vice versa. Achieving balance requires perceiving the rhythm of the cycles of life and our personal cycles.

As our physical bodies rise to a healthier state, we must begin to focus on our mental and emotional states as well. Resentments and ill will may be found gathering dust in the recesses but can be easily identified when they are triggered by situations similar to the originals that created them. This is an ongoing process of seeing, observing, and releasing. Make a game of the challenges. They will come and go.

In the Bible, it often says, "And it came to pass ..." It never says, "And it came to stay."

Have patience to wait out the lows, and try not to cling to the highs.

Think of yourself as an acrobat in the circus, and *remember* that true progress comes when you're having *fun!*

Go Slow to Get There Faster

*O*nce upon a time, there was man who needed to get his pig to the fair. He loaded the sow into his wagon and began the long trek down the mountainside. The dirt road was rocky and yesterday's rain had rutted the mud with puddles and pits. Traveling too slowly he would not arrive before the market gates opened so he decided to drive the horses faster. Soon the horses were pulling the wagon at a furious pace and he was certain he would make it to the fair on time.

Unfortunately, the man's wagon was old and in some disrepair. Hitting a rock, one of its wheels flew off bringing horse, cart and all to a crashing halt. The old man spent the next four hours repairing the wagon, forced to make the rest of the journey at a more cautious speed, causing him to arrive at the fair too late.

The moral of this story is as the title states - *Go Slow to Get There Faster*. This applies to all areas of life. Look at the cars going nowhere in "rush hour" traffic on the "speedway" if you need a present-day reminder.

Our work on our spiritual growth is no exception to this rule. How we wish we could all snap our fingers and our lives would be instantly transformed, but this is not the way it happens on planet earth. Most everything benefits from taking our time to do it correctly. Let there be no contempt for the word "patience" lest the contempt itself set us backward.

Contempt is a negative emotion. Contempt prior to investigation has deprived many a person of the healing they might have experienced had they been more amenable.

Medical science has revealed that contempt felt and/or shown toward another person damages both the sender and receiver's immune systems—another fine example of how dangerous negative emotions are.

Negative emotions and ABSOLUTES corrupt our inner work. When we get stuck in absolutes like "never" and "always" we create many more problems than solutions. Absolutes are almost always guaranteed to manifest opposition —notice I included the word "almost."

Statements like "I will never _____" and "I always _____" challenge life to show us the exceptions. If no personal examples of this come to mind, feel free to experiment. Verification of truth is a big part of this work on self.

Words hold more weight than most of us give them credit. God is said to have created the world with a word. I have no doubt of that probability. Our words are constantly creating our reality. Consider the woman who grew up in the seventies when the catch phrase "Gag me with a pitchfork" (also phrased as "Gag me with a spoon") was popular among high school students. (Though I have no idea who came up with such an absurd statement or why, more than one person I knew used it repeatedly.)

The woman I refer to suffered with chronic episodes of strep throat throughout her high school years and ended up having health issues with her thyroid later in life. Was she, symbolically, being gagged with a pitchfork (or spoon)?

Another high school acquaintance would constantly say, "Can you dig it?" He now shovels graves for a living. Shoveling graves is an admirable job, but a world away from the career as a famous painter that he had envisioned. Another person would use the word "sh*t" in response to just about anything and coincidentally ended up pumping septic tanks for a living—another much needed service in the world, but not his anticipated career.

I once had a neighbor that used a cell

phone that rarely had good reception where she lived. Often there was static during her conversations and people kept telling her, "You're breaking up." She'd broken two phones, three teeth, and hadn't been able to maintain a romantic relationship for several years until she began asking people to recognize that she was not the one "breaking up," that it was the cell signal that was breaking up. She is now happily married, and lives in an area with better cell phone coverage.

Do these stories confirm that words are manifesting destinies? If no personal examples of this come to mind for you, again, feel free to experiment.

I suggest that when spewing out little ditties like, "Give me a break," "You're yanking my chain," "He/she makes me sick," "You're killing me," or "It's to die for," think twice before your lips move and send sound vibrations into the universe.

Slowing down to observe the words you use will make you more aware of the words you choose.

Having the patience to go slower is a work itself. "The reward of patience is patience," accurately describes spiritual growth. When we practice patience, we exercise patience. When we exercise patience, it grows stronger.

We will need patience to proceed forward with our work on reprogramming our programming. We will need it even more when we are in the cycle of backsliding.

Life is full of cycles. Rising and falling, buying and selling, giving and receiving, remembering and forgetting, coming and going. Moving forward and back is another cycle to become aware of in work on oneself. No one, in the beginning, likes backsliding.

Backsliding in our inner work is much like having to stay in bed with the flu or a broken leg. It slows us down. It feels uncomfortable. It interrupts our momentum. It's as if we are molting, shedding the old self and, assuming we don't give up hope and get lost in the process, morphing into a new, more developed person.

When we use backsliding time and any other downtime to review our lessons, we can see that it is actually useful. Like a college exam, we have to review and test ourselves to find out what we have really learned, what we remember, and what areas might still need some scrutiny.

We finally learn to appreciate the ebb with the flow when we start to view them both as equal opportunities to exercise patience and apply the knowledge we have gained.

It all comes back to slowing the cart to better navigate the path. Ecclesiastes 3:1 "To every thing there is a season, and a time to every purpose under the heaven."

Fire in the Furnace

*B*efore we can accomplish these great tasks that lead us out of temptation and toward transformation, we must address the most important concept of all—Passion Management. For, without Passion Management we are hopelessly cast to-and-fro upon the stormy seas of external influences. Distracted and dismayed, we have little chance of connecting with Higher Forces and even less of holding onto that connection.

Passion Management gives us the opportunity to take personal responsibility for our actions and reactions toward external influences. We can learn to *respond* rather than *react.* We can demonstrate *remorse* rather than wallow in *regret.* We can *know* rather than *guess.* We can bring solid resolution to the conflicts that often arise between our head-minds and heart-minds.

This technique of internal conflict-resolution can be successfully applied to external situations as well. Ordinarily, it is so much easier to notice other people's behaviors and our feelings about them, than it is to be aware of our own ego-trips. Passion Management allows us the kind of self-awareness that permeates into all areas of our lives in a positive and meaningful way.

Learning Passion Management is much like performing open-heart surgery on oneself using everyone and everything as a mirror—with no anesthetic. Like everything else in real work on oneself, it is not for those who don't want to *work that hard.* Yet, it is rewarding beyond words for those who are willing to make great efforts to learn and apply it to their lives on a day-by-day, minute-by-minute basis.

When beginning this lesson in Passion Management we start by taking a different view of ourselves. First, we must see that we are all three—the laboratory, the experiment, and the scientist.

We will learn to differentiate between our various parts. The animal part of our nature produces our physical instincts. The inner child deeply affects our emotions. The parental part of our nature lives in our logical mind. The adult well-balanced human that we truly are connects us with our intuition, our subconscious contact with Higher Forces (aka Higher Power, God, Great Spirit, Infinite I, or whatever you opt to call it) with which we eventually begin to have Conscious

Contact through the higher mind.

When we learn to blend and befriend our fabulous three—physical, emotional, and mental —we quickly see how eager our Higher Power is willing to join hands with us in the fiery furnace of our personal transformation.

The Bible story of Daniel's adventures in Babylon is the perfect metaphor for this process. Shadrach, Meshach, and Abednego are tossed into the fiery furnace by the egomaniac King Nebuchadnezzar because they would not worship his material ego-trips, but rather they remained loyal to their spiritual aims. Because of their firm focus on their spiritual aims they were—much to the surprise of the King (ego)—joined in the furnace by a Higher Power. This was a shock to the King (ego) and he was, for that moment, humbled into contemplation of this process.

Such is the humbling of our own ego-mania necessary, which brings us to the subject of how shock and awe assist us in recognizing where self-importance is getting in the way of our progress.

The first shock is our birth into this life. Birth is a huge shock! There we are, nestled in our warm embryonic sac of nutritious fluid, when suddenly we are spat out into the world and cut off from our source of nourishment and comfort.

Bham! Like a lightning strike! We soon forget about this shock, but at the time it is the spark that sets our lives outside of the womb into motion—and a divine spark it is!

Science class teaches us that a spark creates an arc—the stronger the spark, the larger the arc. Fireworks give us a visible view of how this spark and arc process works. Birth, being an enormous shock-spark, creates an enormous life-arc, which can set life into motion or over-whelm it causing a retreat back into the void. Other shocks that come along during our lives can extend our original life-arc or send us into overwhelm and retreat. Near-death experiences offer strong shock-sparks that can often renew our life-arc, although I do not recommend near-death experiences if you can avoid them.

Life will deliver plenty of shock-sparks to wake us up to being present. We can avert some of the harsher of life's shock-sparks by creating our own shock-sparks, which we call "alarm clocks."

To create these types of "alarm clocks" we give ourselves an exercise to do that will shift us from autopilot into presence. If we brush our teeth with our right hand, we use our left hand instead for a few days. We may assign ourselves the task of taking a deep breath when walking through a doorway or turning a key in a lock. We might place a chair in the path we generally take when walking through a room so we have to walk around it for a few days. And so on.

These exercises need to be creative and cause us to pause to think and act differently in order to shift from autopilot to presence. The more present we are, the less life needs to shock us into consciousness. Capiche?

These exercises are not a temporary task. This is a permanent assignment. The ringtone of the alarm clock needs to change every few days. Be creative. You can even set an alarm on your phone to call you to presence once or twice a day, but beware this also may become an autopilot function if used repetitiously. To get an idea of how quickly we fall out of presence try posting a sticky note on your bathroom mirror or refrigerator and observe how many days later you no longer notice it is there. You will see what I mean.

If you will set your own alarm clocks and practice waking yourself up several times a day, you will able to do the following exercise:

Think of something that you need to make a decision about and write it down as a question. Take a piece of paper and draw lines to make three columns. Title the first column EMOTION, the second column LOGIC, and the third INTUITION.

Place your hand on your solar plexus and ask your question aloud. For example, "Should I buy a new car?"

Does the area under your hand tighten? Do you feel an emotion? Do you emotionally desire the new car—or do you emotionally withdraw from the idea? Write your reaction in the EMOTION column.

Next, place your hands on the temples of your head and ask the question aloud again.

Are your temples throbbing? Does your logical mind start crunching the numbers and decide it will cost too much money—or that, yes, it is the logical thing to do to save money, versus all you are spending on repairing your old car or on public transportation? Write your reaction in the LOGIC column.

You have now identified the emotional desires of your inner child versus the demands for security arising from your inner parent. The inner child's purpose is to remind us to play. The inner parent's purpose is to remind us to be safe and secure.

Finally, place your hand on your belly just below your navel. Ask the question aloud once again.

Does the area tighten or relax? Tightening means *do not proceed* or proceed with great caution. Relaxing means proceed with Grace. This is your inner adult—your INTUITION speaking.

Now look at your columns. Does your INTUITION (adult) agree with your EMOTION (child) or LOGIC (parent)? This is where things get a little crazy for most of us. If all three are in agreement, which is rare at best, that is wonderful. More often either your inner child or inner parent is going to have to bite the bullet, and the one that draws the short straw is going to make you pay for rebuffing them unless you do something to make peace before proceeding, or not proceeding, whichever way your intuitive adult is about to move.

Tips for Tots: Children are easily distracted, so if your inner child is the one about to have a tantrum, then your job will be to lovingly embrace and distract him/her. A good movie, an ice cream bar, a trip to the park or the swimming pool—any of these things usually will work. Be creative. As with all children, all will be forgotten and forgiven, quickly and quietly, through tender loving care and distraction.

The poop on Parents: Parents are protective (most are anyway) and concerned with safety and security so distraction is not a technique that will work with your logical parental mind. You must find a way to convince your inner parent that there is sound reasoning to your decision and that safety and security are assured. Having a Plan B that ensures backup is usually enough to assuage the rage of the inner protective parent.

You may think this is nuts, but I guarantee that every time you make a decision that goes against the grain of one or the other, the inner child or inner parent, there will be hurdles they will throw in your way. When you use this method to cover your bases, your path will be smoother. When one or the other is left hanging out in the wind of insecurity there will be hell to pay, road blocks, harassment, and internal conflict that will not let you rest until it is resolved to the satisfaction of the part of you that is being ignored.

Practice this exercise often and be amazed at the inner peace that will result. You will find, however, as most of us inevitably do, that your inner child or inner parent may be challenging to make peace with at times. The reason for this is that there may be deeper levels of resentment buried from past rejections you have bestowed upon them under similar circumstances. In these cases, grab your metaphoric shovel and get ready to do some digging into your psyche.

Our lives are much like nesting dolls—you

know the ones that snap together layer upon layer, growing ever larger with each new snap. If you view these layers as years of your life, you can trace the root causes to the offending year and work to repair that layer. This allows us to move forward less impeded by the past where negative emotions have embedded themselves like fossils in a rock formation.

The releasing of negative emotions is most successful using a combination of breath and awareness. Becoming aware of just how important something or someone is, especially your self, helps to get things into a more realistic perspective. Self-importance is a double-edged sword, however, and we need all be aware that although good, solid self-esteem is necessary to survival, so too is humility. So breathe and release.

Many of us are shallow breathers making it difficult to release negative energies from our bodies on a regular basis. Some are hurdle breathers that breathe fairly well until there is some critical event that takes place in our lives and we tend to stop breathing well until the crisis has passed. Keeping attention on our breathing gives us the opportunity to adjust accordingly to a deeper, smoother breathing style. Meditating daily helps to train our bodies to breathe more steadily.

Just as important as all of these exercises

that help us with Passion Management, is our body's energy level. If you think of a thermostat regulating the temperature in a building you'll easily grasp that when the thermostat is set too low it will get colder and when it's set too high it will overheat. If the pilot light goes out, well, you'd better have a match nearby.

Eastern medicine teaches that anger, rage, and hostility are emotions brought about by too much heat in the liver, or *yang (masculine energy)*, whereas lethargy and depression are symptoms of too much chill in the kidneys, or *yin (feminine energy)*.

We can get "all fired up" or feel "drained"—often when we feel too drained of energy we'll get all fired up to compensate. How many times have you heard someone say, "I lost my temper because I'm depressed." Sadly, when we don't have enough energy to deal with life on life's terms, we will often opt to steal energy from someone else by eliciting their rage or pity. They spew anger back at us or try desperately to console us, spilling their energy in the process and we pull that free energy in. Suddenly our thermostats have been swapped and neither party was privy to what just took place.

This process is a form of "vampirism." Most people are completely unconscious of this process whether they are on one end of the fangs or the other. When we become consciously aware of this behavior in ourselves, and others, we can opt out of vampirism and concentrate on our personal healing and spiritual growth.

Bottom Line: When our physical body is well nourished, our energy level will balance. When our energy level is balanced, our thoughts and feelings are naturally clearer and more positive and optimistic. As a result, it's much easier to be present, and our lives become more manageable. Even during times of illness, loss, and discomfort, we find it's possible to relax and harmonize with acceptance and a genuine gratitude for this gift of True Conscience.

Remember that it's not what is happening, but how we respond to what is happening that establishes our serenity.

It's a Small World After All

*M*illions of egos are running amuck on planet Earth, Sandy. You are one of these egos, and I am another, and there are many others that we will and won't come into contact with in our lives. There will be times that we will find joy in the friendship of others, and other times when the friction between others and us will seem overwhelming to our senses.

It is at this point of friction that those who are addicted to being in control at any cost, may become either suicidal (self-destructive) or homicidal (control-freaking). I use those terms in a generalized manner, for they do not always manifest as fatal. They can and do manifest in various ways under certain conditions. Whether by a loss of attention to the present moment or a loss of self-discipline, they can be detrimental to our health as well as to that of others.

Be it a negative emotion slowly eating away at our physical health and mental well-being, an unfortunate accident caused by inattentiveness, or conscious or unconscious self-sabotaging behavior in our relationships, we may wittingly or unwittingly harm ourselves and/or others to any measure of tragedy.

Escapism can be addictive. Addictive personalities are really dealing with a two part process—the psychological aspect of addiction and the physical aspect of addiction.

When psychologically, we wish to escape our surroundings, our situations, our relationships, our responsibilities, our emotions, etc, it's the path of least resistance that the addictive personality will generally take.

For those who find a mood-altering substance that blows their body, mind and emotions away from the reality they wish to escape, they'll most often reach for that particular substance to "blow them away." In the process, a chemical reaction is taking place in the physical body that causes a shift and/or complete meltdown of the senses that unhinges the person from reality. Some call it "getting high." Some call it "getting low." I call it "getting gone" because we are no longer present when we are in the physiological state of a chemical reaction—we have moved into a state of disconnect—we are "gone."

This ability to use chemical reactions to disconnect from reality can be handy for doctors to use with patients that are in dire physical pain, but can become a wrecking ball for those who use this method to escape everyday reality as often as possible.

Those who are addicted to mood-altering personalities don't have to go to the liquor store, pharmacy or their drug dealer to cop a buzz. The chemical reaction they use to escape is built in—it's called the adrenalin-cortisol reaction. As long as these types of escapists remain in a state of fight-or-flight, the flow of adrenalin and cortisol continues rushing through their systems, keeping them functioning at a purely instinctual level and ascertaining that they are also, essentially, "gone."

The adrenalin-cortisol chemical reaction is extremely useful when a person is in a truly dangerous situation. When facing T-Rex or a mugger in a dark alley, this is the body's natural survival reaction that boosts our ability to run faster (flight) or hit harder (fight). It's the super-power that has enabled humans to survive all these millennia. However, it's so very damaging when these chemical-hormones are constantly coursing through our veins unnecessarily.

What a rush! Chemical reactions help us to escape reality, which is why escapists generally use them—and those who do use them to escape on a regular basis we call "addictive personalities."

Whether physically and/or psychologically addicted to the rush out of reality, addictive personalities do not possess the Real Will to stop the train before it derails.

Self-sabotage leads to derailment. It's a form of suicide, regardless of speed. Addictive personalities often sabotage themselves in their desperate desire to escape the way they are feeling. Whether feeling happy, sad, mad, or confused, really does not matter—escapists just want to change the way they feel.

Isn't that amazing? One would think that feeling healthy and happy wouldn't be a state of mind one would want to change, but this too is an uncomfortable state for the mind of an escapist-addictive personality, for to be still and unchanging for even a moment might permit some exposure of an innermost wound. Escapist-addictive personalities that choose mind-altering substances as a shortcut to short-circuit their present state of heart and mind are practicing self-sabotaging behavior—in a self-destructive, suicidal form.

Likewise, when someone feels a compulsion to control another's opinion or actions, they are often doing so in order to circumvent dealing with their own issues. Focusing on changing others helps to avoid the challenging work of changing ourselves...for a while. So many escapists, so few real doors.

Some self-recovery programs would like to separate all escapists into groups defined by the particular escape route that each finds the most effective. Let's delve deeper to discover the common reasons we choose any mood-or-focus-altering escape route. Some are running away for lack of a known alternative to *kill the pain*, and others are stuck in a mood-or-focus-altering habit on autopilot, using tried and true escape routes to kill *all* feelings including *joy*. When we work in any spiritual development program, it is important to remember that we must not only repair the former, but also reform the latter.

Some programs available for the reformation of addictive personalities focus mainly on controlling mood-altering urges, which is helpful, but their secular notions sometimes prevent us from collectively addressing the common root we all share—escapism. We could confidently gather together a unified group and call it "Escapists Synonymous."

Seldom are we taught as children to recognize our escapist tendencies. Nor are we often given the tools to overcome them while we are young and impressionable. More often, it is only as quasi-grown-ups, when we have driven our lives into a ditch that we finally come stumbling or crawling into a recovery program for relief—at least, those of us that are still alive.

It is appropriate, at this time, to recognize the one viable reason for the secular recovery programs. Very simply, most humans seem to share one singular apparent belief, which we seem to cherish above all others and will cling to with our dying breath—that is the belief that *no one completely understands us.*

After all, how could you possibly understand me if you haven't lived my life, suffered my pain, lived through the horrors and joys of my very personal existence; likewise, I you, you them, etc.

We tend to be particularly protective of our personal treasure chests full of joyful life experiences, yet peculiarly and somewhat awkwardly attached to our personal pain.

What recovery programs have discovered is simply that few experienced alcoholics will well follow the advice of anyone who hasn't, him/herself, struggled with addiction to alcohol. In the same way, few overeaters will listen wholeheartedly to anyone who has never experienced being an overeater. No drug addict will take much stock in what anyone has to say about how to recover from his/her drug addiction when the well-meaning advisor has never had the experience of being addicted to drugs him/herself. No addictive "fixer" of other people's problems will comprehend the advice of someone who hasn't the experience of healing from such a dilemma in their own world; and so on.

Yet, once a person who has "been there, done that" speaks to another person who is "stuck there, doing that," something seems to click and, suddenly, our ears unlock and can hear something helpful.

A terrific example of this is the man who has lived all of his wealthy life in an affluent country, lecturing a man who has lived all of his poverty-stricken life in an impoverished country, about creating an investment portfolio. It's incongruous.

Both men, however, may have been through a painful divorce or may cheer for the same football team, and this shared experience can bring them together in a conversation that puts them on common ground. The subject of disparate finances could cause them to be bitter enemies, whereas their shared common experience in another area of life has the possibility of bonding them in friendship forever.

This commonality is but a beginning, a groundwork laid for a deeper work on oneself.

Having recovered from an addiction to a mood-altering substance, addictive personality types benefit by working together with those who are addicted to mood-altering personalities—those addictive personality types that are addicted to fixing addictive personality types—and vice versa.

Suffering from feeling a lack of control over our lives as well as over the rest of the world, is the common ground between most escapists. Mirroring our experiences helps us to get a good snapshot of the pain that the addict-escapist and/or fixer-escapist knowingly or unknowingly causes the people around him/her. It also increases our understanding of the source of man's natural frustration at not being able to control his/her environment. Ultimately, it presents us with the opportunity to learn healthier ways to change the way we feel, and develop tools to feel more comfortable with feelings of discomfort.

The real, albeit sometimes painful, truth is that discomfort often actually benefits us by sticking around until we get the lesson it offers. It is the fuel-source of burning desire and, consequently, effective change. Learning to let go in Grace begins with the burning desire to do so and the right guidance to assist.

The motto of a practicing escapist addicted to mood-altering substances—"I want to change the way **I** feel." The motto of a practicing escapist using other people's problems to cast shadows on his/her own—"I want to change the way **you** feel." We often imagine that if the other person would just change the way he/she feels and behaves, then we would all live happily ever after. *And*... the chase is on, with everyone running away from their perceived ills and toward their debilitating dis-eases.

If one is looking to master one's addictive programming, the chain-smoking, sugar-aholic, caffeine addict still practicing self-destructive behavior with but a change of poisons, is not probably the best guide. Nicotine, caffeine, sugar, and the like, taken in excess, are just as damaging to the body and mind as alcohol, street drugs, and pharmaceuticals taken in the same manner.

To work on the whole enchilada, it is necessary to work with someone who is working on his/her own whole enchilada. Someone looking to work only the corners of the puzzle may find this frustrating, however we who succeed do so because we comprehend that half efforts avail us nothing. We will never know if there were some shades of hypocrisy in the spiritual teachings of those who came before us—they were only human, as are we all, and I'm sure, if so, they made up their own excuses, as we all do, however it's our duty as a new generation to reach higher.

The justification that most people use for substituting one destructive behavior for another, or only addressing one destructive behavior rather than the whole ball of wax, usually sounds something like this: "I can only deal with one addiction at a time." That there, my friend, is a prime example of irrational rationalizing in all its glory. How easily we deceive ourselves when we simply don't want to *work that hard*.

We wander through life under the influence of self-deception, and we step on the toes of many while blaming them for putting their feet in our way—or, we may be so focused on the other guy stepping on our own sore toes that we miss our own shortcomings entirely.

Who is objective enough in and of one's self to be thoroughly accountable to only one's self? The Christ? The Buddha? Not even them, as they made themselves accountable to All and Everything.

One of the sweetest gifts that a spiritual recovery/discovery program offers is that nearly everywhere we travel there is someone else like us, struggling to make sense of life, the universe and everything. Around each corner, someone else like us is waiting to share a "hello" and shine the light of a knowing smile, ever reminding us that it is a small world after all and we are accountable to the whole of it should we be that humble.

Should we not yet be that humble, then igniting our burning desire and asking our Higher Power for guidance toward someone who can provide solid accountability for us is paramount.

There is no great abyss that abiding faith can't shrink down to size.

High Tide at the Okeedokee Corral

They say that the closer we get to the light, the more aware of the darkness we become. Isn't it interesting that at high noon we cast no shadows? Might that be relative to our inner light in the sense that, when we make efforts to remain centered in love, negative emotions simply don't exist, just as our shadows are nowhere to be seen when the sun shines straight down upon us?

These states are, once again, cyclical in nature. The sun rises and sets, you say, but, in fact, the sun does not rise or set; it is we who turn toward the sun and, then away. Could it be just as true for us that it is not the love that rises and sets for us, but, that we turn toward and then away from love, while thinking all along that it is the love that chooses or eludes us?

Just as the moon reflects the light of the sun, we too reflect the spiritual light of our Higher Power. Just as the moon pulls the tides of the oceans, we too, consisting of mostly water are pushed and pulled by this lunar influence. The tides of the oceans crash upon smooth or rocky shores, while the tides of our emotions crash upon smooth or rocky situations or people.

Though to overcome the moon and stars may be a bit beyond our capabilities, we can aspire toward more down-to-earth virtues. When peer pressure tempts us to wander from our aim to heal, can we hold our ground or are we swayed? When unhealthy habits beckon to take the wheel, can we hold fast or do we yield the driver's seat?

When we are given the choice between exemplifying Hope, Faith, and Love that might inspire the people around us to be aroused and awaken, or joining the ones in the sleep state of unhealthy behavior, will we choose to be a mountain of stability or a grain of sand swept beneath the wave?

Our peers and patterns ought not to have power over our destiny. Somewhere down the line, if we begin to look more honestly at ourselves, we may see the light. It may occur to us that we have been a tad irresponsible, disrespectful, and possibly even downright self-indulgent in our past, and it might inspire us to work toward improving our internal affairs for a better, brighter tomorrow.

While we cannot control the moon, lunar

influences are still important to explore as they can inspire *lunatics* to *lunacy.* Look around you during any full moon and the evidence is over-whelming. Hospital emergency rooms overflow, obstetricians can barely keep up with mothers birthing their babies, and the sirens of police, fire, and ambulance vehicles fill the air.

Dreams fulfilled pervade the world with joy at the full moon time as well. When we are balanced and whole, we can wish and our wishes can come to fruition. Like the cycles of the moon, our fulfillment has its own cycles.

I once knew an old woman who would go outside late at night during full moons wearing shamrock pajamas, and run around her yard with a big paper bag scooping moonbeams. She said that the moon filled her bag with good luck and wishes come true.

An old proverb says, "Be careful what you wish for as you just might get it." One thing is certain, when what we wish finally manifests it will be in God's time, not necessarily ours, so prac-ticing patience with our cycles bodes well for our serenity.

Let the Sunlight of the Spirit infuse you with peace and joy. Let the light of Grandmother Moon empty your ego and fill you with new dreams as she waxes and wanes.

Let your life be one of flowing with the rhythm of Love as it moves through you like a river, some parts calm, some parts rapid, yet moving ever onward toward the sea. Become aware of the tide within you. Learn when to surf and when to rest.

Be on guard that your energy is not lost on negative emotions, conflict, and ego-trips. Like the earth corrals and channels its water from the mountaintops, through the rivers, on into the ocean, corral and channel your energy into positive thoughts, balanced emotions, and productive deeds.

We may come to our burning desire through a total eclipse of the heart, but the sun can and will shine again. Let the light of Faith, Love, and Hope grow within you that you may shine the way for others to follow.

Reflect to the world all the love in your heart and grow with the flow, Sandy. Okeedokee?

Keep It Simple Sweetie

$\mathscr{I}$ have heard many people speak about their struggles toward reaching a Spiritual Awakening. Twelve Step programs try to describe it in the eleventh step; many religions attempt to define it; metaphysicians often speak abstractly about it; and rudimentary scientists try to debunk the possibility of such a thing as a Spiritual Awakening.

Mostly, I believe, the semantics get in the way. When we talk about the "psychic change" and "spiritual awakening" that we must work to attain, I wonder, is it really as mysterious as it sounds?

Simplicity is the great de-mystifier of the universe. Much to the discontent of those who enjoy the attention received when stumbling and bumbling around a thing, and those who would profess from their pulpits and podiums that they alone hold the key to the great and mysterious, I say, "Hogwash."

Keep it simple sweetie: Follow the steps of reprogramming; and when the new programming overrides the old programming, and we finally find ourselves doing the next right thing naturally, this is evidence of the "psychic change" taking place in us. There is nothing spooky or mysterious about a perfectly natural chemical process that comes built-in and flows unpretentiously when you shine the light of simplicity on it.

The "Spiritual Awakening" that we work so hard to try to analyze and understand is simply *seeing* ourselves in this moment of "psychic change" and enjoying the "WOW!" Seeing ourselves through God's eyes is miraculous!

To put it in even simpler terms—it's called "Growing Up." We, quite literally, mature physically, emotionally, and mentally; and when we do that, we cannot help but unearth a great chemical change within. The words we use, like "psychic" and "spiritual" are the things that seem to cause the confusion we hear and sometimes feel among the troops internally as well as externally.

Let's look at this whole process from front to back: Break Down, Break Through, Break Free.

Tend to your physical, emotional, and mental health. Unless you have a physical disability that prevents you from moving your body, get into gear.

Are you stuck emotionally? Stuck mentally?

You've got to *moove-it, moove-it, moove-it*. Physical movement will get you unstuck fast. Walk, run, bike, hike, swim, ski, dance, jump, hop, skip, clean house; just do something physically active!

Get plenty of sunshine and fresh air. Eat healthy foods and get the right nutrition. Your body is like a machine and just as a car needs oil and gas to keep its engine running efficiently, you need a healthy diet rich with the proper proteins, vitamins and minerals, etc, to keep your body running smoothly.

Your body also needs rest, so get your beauty sleep and take catnaps when you need them; and make time to sit still in meditation.

Another part of your routine physical maintenance is steering clear of toxic chemicals. For your body's sake, don't put sugar in your fuel tank—literally, as refined sugar has been proven to have negative effects on automobiles as well the human body. Few sugar substitutes are any better.

Learn to read labels, scary as that may prove to be. A friend of mine taught me to read the ingredients on everything I buy. She said that if a possibly tasty item on the grocery store shelf has more than five ingredients and you can't pronounce one or more of them, or don't know what they are, don't buy it, and definitely don't eat it. Given the amounts of antibiotics, hormones, pesticides, preservatives, artificial colors and flavorings added to our food supply in today's age, her words of wisdom are worth paying forward.

Our bodies need a good supply of fresh water. Some medical professionals say that we should divide our body weight in half and convert that number to ounces to find out how much water we should be drinking daily. This obviously will vary for different body types with different health issues. Nevertheless, a good intake of water not only keeps our tank full, but also flushes out toxic chemicals that might otherwise become detrimental to our health down the line.

Keep a clean digestive system. If you have problems digesting the food you put into your physical body how will your mind and emotions be able to digest your life experiences any better?

When the body—the Physical Self—is nurtured and balanced, then our moods—the Emotional Self—tend to follow suit. It is easier to be calm and joyful when we feel healthy.

If our emotions continue crashing against the rocky shores of life, there is still something physically amiss. Before reaching for pharmaceuticals, we can explore a variety of nutritional options. Many health professionals have come to understand us as whole human beings, and have written at length about various options we have available to help get our physical bodies up to their optimal healthy states.

Pharmaceuticals may, for some, become temporarily or permanently necessary, so it is important not to rule them out altogether. You should be able to rely on the advice of an educated professional such as your trusted physician to discern when and where it is time to draw a line in the sand.

Hugs—get lots of them and give lots of them. *Everything we are benefits from hugs.* We are living, breathing human beings that need to share the love! Multiple tests on the human brain have proven the profoundly favorable effects that a simple hug provides to our state of being.

Humility is a must. Be always willing to acknowledge that you alone are *not* the mightiest force in the universe. Self-reliance is a giraffe in stiletto heels walking a tightrope—head held high and nowhere to go but down.

Embody an attitude of gratitude. Having a grateful heart for the miracles in life, both small and large, and appreciating the guidance offered keeps the gifts rolling in.

Self-observation will reveal patterns and habits that need reconditioning. Do not let accurate observations turn into inaccurate judgments about them. The mind can twist things if you are not observing it also.

Some folk get confused between what is *mental* and what is *intellectual*, so let's get clear about these two terms. For our purposes, "Mental" is the *state of mind* we are in and out of, whereas "Intellect" is more related to the *cognitive processes* of our brains. Regardless of whether we have the cognitive abilities of Einstein or a fruit fly, we still must deal with our fluctuating states of mind—the Mental Self.

In my life-long search for truth and wisdom, I've found nothing more balancing for the mind than physical exercise, prayer and meditation—moving in rhythm and, then, simply sitting quietly and still long enough to allow the amazing chemical processes natural to all human beings to do the work of defragmenting our mental and intellectual hard drives.

When the physical body is healthy and the emotions are calm, the mind unwinds, and the central nervous system is restored, returning harmony to the Whole Self.

Although I am not a fatalist, I do believe in a kind of personal destiny as well as an evolutionary kind of cyclical destiny that keeps the cosmic wheels of our universe turning. The consistency of the rules of our universe, such as the law of cause-and-effect and the rule of probability, is more and more visible to me as my efforts to see beyond the ego increase. It's clear that we are made of more than flesh and bone alone.

Striving for optimal physical health is important, even for those of us who will never be star athletes or may even be on our way out of our bodies, altogether. Many of us come into our lives with physical challenges or manage to acquire them along the way. They can prevent us from feeling healthy and strong despite all efforts to be "cured" of them. This is no excuse to drop the ball and give in to the ego's urge to abandon our journey toward awakening to a higher level of consciousness. Quite the opposite, this type of "fierce grace"—as my soul-friend Ram Dass refers to it—is simply the gift of a built-in alarm clock relentlessly calling us to choose consciousness over and above negative emotions like self-pity, depression, or rage. We would be foolish to cause ourselves unnecessary pain or invite dis-ease into our lives, however when we are confronted with either we benefit by turning the experience into something useful for our spiritual growth.

Some of us will use these challenges

wisely, and some will not. It will depend on whether genuine joy and faith reside strongly, deeply within us, or our happiness and state of well-being are solely dependent on external influences. If our egos are constantly in distress over what others are doing or thinking about us there is no time or space for our souls to be present. If we are always wrestling with physical or emotional anxiety and pain, we will find no inner peace until we learn to let go of the ego's attachment to it.

Dealing with personal health issues of a physiological nature can be discouraging. Coping with our emotions as we watch loved ones pass through illness or death can be disheartening. Striving for balance on a churning ocean is a daunting task when we perceive our experience through the eyes of the ego. From the stillness of our soul's perspective, however, we can turn our attention toward True Conscience and connect with higher forces where true comfort welcomes us.

Faith is not an attribute of the ego; it's solely a soul experience. For those who don't believe in the existence of such a thing as a "soul"—*as surely as wherever the darkness is not, there you will find the light; wherever the ego is not, there you will find the soul.*

It matters not nearly as much *that* we live as *how* we live.

We could continue to expound on the vast amount of information discovered and redis- covered throughout time immemorial regarding the workings of the soul with the self—physical, emotional, and mental—and how we function as parts and together, but that would be defeating our purpose to Keep It Simple Sweetie, so let it go. Stay focused on the task-at-hand. Hmmm...

In this busy-bee era, the concept of "letting go" has somehow gone from releasing ourselves from struggle to becoming a struggle unto itself. There is a Zen proverb that says, "It is not what we carry with us, but what we let go, that defines who we are." On this path toward Spiritual Awakening, we learn to let go of that which no longer serves us, and mature into a person who exemplifies a new, healthier manner of living and loving.

We learn to be the watcher of our own behaviors and to trace their origins. We learn to ask for help with reprogramming our program- ming; and we learn that we are far too subjective to be accountable to our own selves without an outside opinion to call upon for more objectivity.

At length, we learn to *become* True

Conscience, to *become* the bridge to our Higher Power. Coming again as little children, pure of heart, we learn how to share this Faith, Hope, and Love with all of the other children we meet on the playground of life.

Here is Wisdom: *Before you can truly help another, Know Thyself.* Each day begin at the beginning. Each night give thanks for each day.

As you stand on the twelfth step, Sandy, the step that will keep your butt up off the floor, I offer this gift of my experience, strength, and hope to carry you into the future. May you pay it forward in the natural rhythms and cycles that your Higher Power will reveal to you, as one and then another and another person enters your life, each with a burning desire to climb this stairway toward Heaven.

Reach out and open your hand, without expectation, without judgment, and without hes-itation, and be lifted higher and higher by those you touch with this truth, as I have been lifted by you.

May you feel my hand in yours always and everywhere.

And so we begin ...

Note to self:

Welcome to the Abyss.

FALL, FLOAT, OR FLY.

You get to Choose.

COMPANION WORK GUIDE

*M*any authors prefer to sell their companion work books separately. I've chosen to include the Dear Sandy companion work guide as a part of this publication for those who wish to start right in on the work. Those with a burning desire for oneness within and without, and are ready and willing to *work that hard,* will probably appreciate the immediate gratification of being able to dive right in!

The following pages contain worksheets to apply the Dear Sandy work-on-self exercises to your personal life in a practical, revelatory, and fun way. Each exercise is relative to one or more chapters in this letter-turned-book so you can review the corresponding chapter(s) as you do the hands-on tasks in this companion work guide.

Each exercise has directions and some have questions to answer. Using this work guide every day will help you see your daily patterns and graph improvements as you grow from day to day and month to month.

Overall, I wish you many successful revelations and a happy new, reprogrammed you!

MEDITATION EXERCISES

Anyone can do an internet search for "meditation exercises" and find hundreds of web sites offering different types of meditations; however, for our purposes we are going to use very specific meditation instructions.

(1)
MEDITATING FOR MASTERY OF THE PHYSICAL STATE

Sitting erect in silence, challenge the body to sit perfectly still without movement of any kind.

For this meditation exercise, you can sit upright in a chair or lotus style on the floor, couch, bed, on a rock outcropping, in the grass in your backyard, etc. You can park yourself on a pillow or Zafu for comfort or you can use a meditation bench or Seiza bench. It's important to position yourself so that your spine is erect and aligned with the center of the earth below you and universe above.

Once in position, close your eyes and begin to focus on your breath. Notice how you are breathing—you may notice that you're taking short breaths, long breaths, or somewhat irregular breaths. Simply notice and stay with your breath for a few moments.

When you are ready, take three slow, deep breaths—inhaling through the nose and exhaling through the mouth, expanding your belly as you breathe in and relaxing as you breathe out.

Close your mouth now and place your tongue on the roof of your mouth using a slight suction to keep it in place. Now you are ready to concentrate on breathing nice even breaths through only your nose. (If you have a condition that prevents breathing through your nose, simply relax your jaw and use mouth breathing for this meditation.)

As you sit with your attention on your breath, you may discover that your body experiences some involuntary movements. Certain areas might twitch or start to itch. Little aches and pains may appear to intensify. For this exercise, your aim is to continue to focus on your breath until the twitching, itching, or pain dissolves from your consciousness.

Don't be discouraged if it takes a week or two before you can begin resisting the intense urge to scratch an itch, or the twitching settles down in your eyelids or other areas of your body, or the aches or pains become dissolvable.

This is a very helpful meditation for those who suffer from chronic pain of any kind. As we steady and pull our attention more deeply into the breath, our bodies slip into relaxation, allowing our consciousness to expand. It's this expansion of our consciousness that shrinks the pain and has the power to dissolve it.

If random thoughts make it difficult for you to start or stay with this meditation, simply place a small notepad and pencil or pen in front of you in your meditative position and close your eyes. When the inner talking begins, open your eyes and write out the words that your mind is chattering. If you start thinking about how you feel emotionally about a certain person or situation, write it down. If your to-do list is nagging you, then write it all down. Allow yourself five minutes to do this mental purging. You can then restart your timer and announce to your mind that the next ten minutes (or longer) belong to your body for its healing. All future chatter ought to be ignored, bringing your attention back to the breath each time it tries to wander to the mind.

You might try doing this meditation for 10 minutes at the start and, after some weeks of practice, gradually increasing the time incrementally to 40 minutes.

NOTES

_____

_____

_____

_____

_____

_____

_____

_____

_____

_____

_____

_____

_____

_____

_____

(2)

MEDITATING FOR MASTERY OF
THE EMOTIONAL STATE

This meditation is done when feeling strong emotion—anger, frustration, grief, shame, and even joy. Physical movement such as walking, running, scrubbing the shower or some other deep cleaning that requires physical movement helps to calm the emotional self. Practicing stillness, in order to completely feel and acknowledge the emotion in your body so that you can learn how to use consciousness to tame this magnificent wild horse, is the aim of this meditation.

Part of Passion Management is getting to know how and where passion moves through your body. Passion is a driving force that energizes us. Just as we can blow up the engine of our automobile if we try to drive faster than our engine is calibrated to go, passion can burn out parts of our physical body if it exceeds the limits of what our body can handle. Expanding our consciousness helps manage the intensity of our passion so our emotional self can feel our life experiences in a way that maintains a healthy balance in our whole Self.

For this meditation exercise, you can sit upright in a chair or lotus style on the floor, couch, bed, on a rock outcropping, in the grass in your backyard, etc. You can park yourself on a pillow or Zafu for comfort or you can use a meditation bench or Seiza bench. It's important to position yourself so that your spine is erect and aligned with the center of the earth below you and universe above.

Once in position, close your eyes and begin to focus on your breath. Notice how you are breath-ing—you may notice that you're taking short breaths, long breaths, or somewhat irregular breaths. Simply notice and stay with your breath for a few moments.

When you are ready, take three slow, deep breaths—inhaling through the nose and exhaling through the mouth, expanding your belly as you breathe in and relaxing as you breathe out.

Close your mouth now and place your tongue on the roof of your mouth using a slight suction to keep it in place. Now you are ready to concentrate on breathing nice even breaths through only your nose. (If you have a condition that prevents breathing through your nose, simply relax your jaw and use mouth breathing for this meditation.)

As you sit with your attention on your breath, you may discover that your body experiences some involuntary movements, the mental chatter may be quite loud, and you experience the intense urge to scream and/or get up and run away. For this exercise, your aim is to continue to focus on your breath until the intensity of these sensations dissolve from your consciousness.

In the beginning, it's best to try this sitting medi-tation only after you've used movement to let off some of the steam so you can actually tune in during the sitting meditation.

The object of this meditation is to observe that **you are not the emotion**. The emotion is driven, i.e.: intensified, by your ego's attachment to it. As your body relaxes into a steady, flowing breath, your consciousness expands and the ego releases its hold. When this happens, we can experience the emotion in a healthy way.

Don't be discouraged. Most of us find it takes years of practicing this meditation before we can begin resisting the intense urge to scrap the whole endeavor. Human beings are designed to feel emotions. We do have a choice, however, whether to allow those feelings to control our lives, or strive to invite a higher state of consciousness to put them in perspective.

You might try doing this meditation for 10 minutes at the start and, after some weeks of practice, gradually increasing the time incrementally to 40 minutes.

NOTES

_____

_____

_____

_____

_____

_____

_____

_____

_____

_____

_____

_____

_____

_____

(3)
MEDITATING FOR MASTERY OF
THE MENTAL STATE

Sitting erect in silence, challenge the mind to be silent.

For this meditation exercise, you can sit upright in a chair or lotus style on the floor, couch, bed, on a rock outcropping, in the grass in your backyard, etc. You can park yourself on a pillow or Zafu for comfort or you can use a meditation bench or Seiza bench. It's important to position yourself so that your spine is erect and aligned with the center of the earth below you and universe above.

Once in position, close your eyes and begin to focus on your breath. Notice how you are breathing—you may notice that you're taking short breaths, long breaths, or somewhat irregular breaths. Simply notice and stay with your breath for a few moments.

When you are ready, take three slow, deep breaths—inhaling through the nose and exhaling through the mouth, expanding your belly as you breathe in and relaxing as you breathe out.

Close your mouth now and place your tongue on the roof of your mouth using a slight suction to keep it in place. Now you are ready to concentrate on breathing nice even breaths through only your nose. (If you have a condition that prevents breathing through your nose, simply relax your jaw and use mouth breathing for this meditation.)

Focus your mind on your body. Begin by placing your attention on the left foot, then moving attention upward to the lower left leg, knee, thigh, hip, then repeating on the right side, starting with the right foot, following up the leg to the hip.

From the hips, channel the flow of your attention into the lower torso, on up through the mid and upper torso all the way to the neck.

From the neck, bring your attention to the left shoulder and flow attention down through the left arm to the hand and on into the fingertips. Repeat for the right arm. Returning to the neck, allow your attention to spread and wrap around the back of the head, as if a hand was slowing cupping and embracing the skull. You should feel your scalp tingling with energy.

Allow your attention to then flow over the top of the head, into your forehead, and down through your face, as a gentle waterfall would wash downward through your facial muscles, relaxing each facial muscle all the way down to your neck.

Begin again at the feet and repeat this flow of attention through your body seven times, slowly.

You might try doing this meditation for 10 minutes at the start and, after some weeks of practice, gradually increasing the time incrementally to 40 minutes.

NOTES

_____

_____

_____

_____

_____

_____

_____

_____

_____

_____

_____

(4)
Meditating for Mastery of Alignment

Once you have Meditations 1, 2 and 3 increased up to at least 30 minutes each, try blending them into one perfect meditation to be done daily in the morning and/or evening hours, preferably at sunrise, and/or at sunset.

You might try doing this blended meditation for 10 minutes at the start and, after some weeks of practice, gradually increasing the time incrementally to 40 minutes.

NOTES

_____

_____

_____

_____

_____

_____

_____

_____

_____

_____

(5)
MEDITATING FOR VIBRATIONAL ATTUNEMENT

Our bodies are powered by electromagnetic energy; therefore we vibrate at a specific frequency. If that frequency drops too low or rises too high, the parts that make up our whole selves are thrown out of sync with each other and we become out of tune with the universe's field of energy. Side effects of being "out of sync" or "out of tune" are usually not fun and can be fatal.

Electromagnetic energy combines electricity and magnetism. For our purpose, we'll simplify our definitions. We possess and are surrounded by magnetic fields. These fields pull on and push around the electrical particles inside and outside of us. Voltage, for our purpose, can be described as the shock-spark—the *Affirming Force*. Current, for our purpose, can be described the life-arc—the *Flow of Energy*. Resistance (the stuff that creates limitation, for better or worse)—the *Resisting Force*, for our purpose, is what we can use to maintain a healthy electromagnetic vibration/frequency.

Interestingly, Electrical Resistance is measured in OHMs.

Like electricians must use Resistance to maintain the flow of a balanced current through the wires in our homes so they don't burn out or burn down, we use our own type of resistance to stay "in sync" and "in tune." Conscious use of the Resisting Force is extremely beneficial to our work on oneself, which is what makes this next meditation exercise so fascinating and so important.

OM... Sitting erect, cover both ears with cupped hands, pressing gently until you can hear the sounds of your blood circulating, heart beating, and lungs inhaling and exhaling. Imagine this is the sound of the Universe. Now open your mouth in the O position, inhale deeply and "OM" on the exhale, making the "OM" (Ah-uommmmmmm) sound to attune your vibration. Repeat this "Breath and OM" three times. Relax into attunement.

You might try doing this vibrational attunement meditation several times a day as it takes only a few minutes.

NOTES

Sweete Notes

NOTE 1: All meditations outlined in this companion work guide should be experienced in the purest silence possible, with no accompanying music or mayhem. Effort should be made to not be distracted by, but to be aware of the sounds of your natural environment, such as birds chirping, dogs barking, cars driving by, etc.

NOTE 2: All meditations outlined in this companion work guide are "Sitting Meditations." They are not "Moving Meditations" such as walking or dancing meditations. Meditating while operating machinery, small or large, is not recommended or advisable—don't do it.

NOTE 3: Although the meditations outlined in this companion work guide are "Sitting Meditations," they can be done lying down if it is not physically possible for the person to sit upright. For those physically capable of sitting upright, doing these meditations in the lying position would be just that—lying.

Up-Down Cycle Exercises

1) **List three examples** of something exciting happening in your life that caused you to feel exceptionally "up" along with something that happened shortly thereafter that caused you to feel the sensation of coming back "down." Here are three examples to study:

Kelly's Example -
This happened that caused me to feel uplifted:

I won $50 on a scratch lottery ticket on a Monday.

This happened that caused me to feel brought back down:

I went to cash in the winning lottery ticket on Tuesday, and got into a fender bender accident in the parking lot, which cost $55 to pay the traffic citation and raised my annual car insurance rates going forward.

Greg's Example -
This happened that caused me to feel uplifted:

I got a promotion at work on Wednesday.

This happened that caused me to feel brought back down:

I received a phone call on Thursday letting me know that a friend had passed on.

Ryan's Example -
This happened that caused me to feel uplifted:

I got a great deal at the nursery on a Friday and was able to purchase two cherry trees for the price of one.

This happened that caused me to feel brought back down:

I planted the cherry trees over the weekend and they looked beautiful, but by mid-week, one of them died for no known reason.

These kinds of things happen to real people in real life. The pendulum swings or time would stand still. Not every up and down are related to each other like in examples numbers one and three. Sometimes we experience events that are unrelated such as in example number two.

Nevertheless, the ups and downs consistently follow each other like a roller coaster ride. Now let's look at the reverse.

2) LIST THREE EXAMPLES of something difficult happening in your life that caused you to feel exceptionally "down" along with something that happened shortly thereafter that caused you to feel the sensation of coming back "up." Here are three examples to study:

Sherry's Example -
This happened that caused me to feel brought down and maybe even a little sad, mad, or depressed:

I found out on a Monday that my best friend had an affair with my husband.

This happened that caused me to feel uplifted:

I won $100,000 in the lottery a few days later.

Taylor's Example -
This happened that caused me to feel brought down and maybe even a little sad, mad, or depressed:

I lost my job in November due to down-sizing at the company.

This happened that caused me to feel uplifted:

I was offered a high-level position with better pay in a completely different industry four weeks later in December.

Mariel's Example -
This happened that caused me to feel brought down and maybe even a little sad, mad, or depressed:

I learned on a Friday that my grandfather was diagnosed with a terminal illness.

This happened that caused me to feel uplifted:

I learned the following Monday that I was pregnant after years of trying to be.

You can see that what goes up does come down and what goes down does come up. To discern which came first is like asking which came first, the chicken or the egg—philosophical distraction. However, it can be very interesting to start observing the upswings and downswings in your life that reveal how life itself manages to balance the scales at all times. Sometimes this balance happens quickly and sometimes it can take weeks, months, or even years. The scales always balance eventually—the pendulum swings in search of its center point.

This awareness is very helpful when things seem to be on the downswing because we can remember that it is only a matter of time before Newton's Third Law of Motion, "For every action there is an equal and opposite reaction," causes things to swing upward once again. Likewise, it is wise to understand that going up too far, too fast will be followed by an equal balancing downward pull.

Meditation helps to bring balance to us internally so that our responses to life's ups and downs don't have to be so intense and stressful.

NOTES

Victim vs. Volunteer Exercises

1) LIST THREE EXAMPLES of a situation in which you were powerless to control the outcome; list what you later discovered was the corresponding purpose, or lesson, for the original situation. Here are three examples to study:

Kip's Example -
I was powerless to control this experience:

I had to close my business due to an unexpected illness during which I was unable to work for six months.

I ultimately learned the purpose/lesson offered by the experience:

I learned that my physical body, no matter how healthy to start with, could not remain healthy under the stress of working eighty hours per week, and how important it is to honor my body's limitations as I grow older even if my mind thinks I'm still a teenager.

Brenda's Example -
I was powerless to control this experience:

My spouse passed on suddenly, leaving me to raise two children on my own.

I ultimately learned the purpose/lesson offered by the experience:

I learned to reach beyond my self-reliant attitude to be grateful for help offered by others rather than feeling like a failure when not being able to do everything all by myself. I also learned how important it is to help others in need as well as to be compassionate with those who find it difficult to ask for help or accept it.

Becky's Example -
I was powerless to control this experience:

A well-respected person in our community in whom I had trusted a confidence, betrayed that trust by not only making my personal matter public but also weaving fabricated untruths into it.

I ultimately learned the purpose/lesson offered by the experience:

I learned to be more cautious about sharing confidences and to be mindful of my own tendencies to gossip about others.

Thomas's Example -
I was powerless to control this experience:

l had only owned my new sports car for two weeks when a friend who had borrowed it, wrecked it while driving too fast.

I ultimately learned the purpose/lesson offered by the experience:

l learned not to loan my possessions to others with an expectation that they will be as caring with them as l would be, and to be mindful of caring well for things loaned to me by others.

List three of your own experiences that you were powerless to control and the lessons you learned from those experiences. What did you learn about yourself? What was your part in the experience? What were your reactions to it? How can you better exercise compassion toward yourself and others when moving through the shock-sparks of life?

NOTES

WORKING WITH THE OCTAVE

"Why" is a question that ought only be asked by a person who is honest, open, and willing to do the work of serious self-inquiry and self-discovery. Reprogramming our inner selves requires asking "Why" and doing this inner work with sincerity of purpose.

The Octave of Understanding is a method that nature has provided to streamline the process of achieving deeper levels of self-discovery, and is outlined here for you to experiment with.

In music, DO-RE-MI-FA-SO-LA-SI are the seven steps that lead to the next higher octave—a higher DO. Once we reach the higher DO, the octave then begins again on this higher level. In music there are two half-steps, or *intervals*, in the octave—the first half-step, or *interval*, is between MI and FA, the second is between SI and the new DO. We can apply the octave to anything in life.

In the Octave of Intention, DO is our intention to begin to *"do"* something. RE—*Revving Energy*—is momentum picking up. MI—*Mechanical Inertia*—is where we reach our first plateau (1st interval), and is the first place we can falter due to complacency or just plain giving up. If, however, we re-invigorate our original intention and assert extra efforts to combat complacency and/or lack of initiative to overcome challenges, we can get ourselves over that little bump in the road and move on to FA—*Further Action*—which renews our perseverance.

SO—*Self-Observation*—requires repetitive patience and awareness. LA requires we *Look At* the bigger picture. SI requires that we *Surrender It* to a Higher Power as this is the turning point (2nd interval) where only higher forces can lift us over the hump to the next higher octave. (For those who prefer "TI" to "SI"—consider TI to be *Trust It* to a Higher Power.)

The Octave of Understanding works in much the same way as the Octave of Intention. To apply the Octave of Understanding to reprogramming our inner programming is transformational! Like an Octave of Intention, the Octave of Understanding allows us to see a more complete picture of the internal programming that is running the show. Review the two examples in the chapter "Lest We Come Again As Little Children." Use the attached worksheet to identify where your three bodies are out of sync and your attention is being misdirected.

Discover what root condition is impeding your passage through the intervals to reach higher levels.

OCTAVE OF UNDERSTANDING WORKSHEET

1) PHYSICAL STATE: What is happening in your physical body lately? How is it feeling? Has it been hurt recently? Damaged? Sick? Chronic? Clumsy? Tired? Is it trying to "get your attention?"

PROBLEM –

_____

_____

_____

_____

SOLUTION –

_____

_____

_____

_____

2) EMOTIONAL STATE: What negative emotions are you feeling lately? Resentment? Anger? Frustration? Jealousy? Loneliness? Sadness? Is there a specific person or situation involved? Is it trying to "get your attention?"

PROBLEM -

_____

_____

_____

_____

SOLUTION -

_____

_____

_____

_____

3) MENTAL STATE: What thoughts are recurring in your mind lately? Thoughts about the past? About the future? About how you are feeling physically? About how you are feeling emotionally? Is it trying to "get your attention?"

PROBLEM -

_____

_____

_____

_____

SOLUTION -

_____

_____

_____

_____

4) ALIGNMENT STATE: Look at numbers 1, 2, and 3—which one(s) are going in different directions? Think of them as tires on a car—are they aligned? Is your attention focused on the present moment or is your mind (#3) on something else?

PROBLEM -

_____

_____

_____

_____

SOLUTION -

_____

_____

_____

_____

5) SELF-AWARENESS STATE: Having identified the underlying condition of your misalignment, assign yourself the task of observing how often and in what areas this is happening in your daily life. You may discover the (#6) root condition (key feature) in a week or it may take longer. Be patient, observant, and thorough.

PROBLEM -

_____

_____

_____

_____

SOLUTION -

_____

_____

_____

_____

6) CLARIFYING STATE: Having observed your underlying condition of misaligned attention and observed its directionality in action in your life, you can now look deeper to identify what programming has been preventing the alignment of your attention.

PROBLEM -

_____

_____

_____

_____

SOLUTION -

_____

_____

_____

_____

7) PRE-CONSCIENCE STATE: Practice accepting the price of experiencing the hot discomfort of burning desire in exchange for genuine contact with a Higher Power. The higher our personal vibration rises, the closer to Higher Forces we get. Lotion up—the heat is on!

PROBLEM—time spent baking in a state of burning desire feels damned uncomfortable;

SOLUTION—get comfortable being uncomfortable, and use prayer and meditation to ask higher forces for assistance.

NOTES

_____

_____

_____

_____

_____

_____

_____

More Exercises For You

Humble vs. Humiliation Exercises

1) List 3 examples of a situation in which you felt humiliated that woke you up to learn something important about yourself. How did you magnetize the situation to you? How did you react to it at the time? What could you have done differently? How did it benefit your inner development in the long run?

2) List 3 examples of a situation in which you took the initiative to humble your own ego and consequently avoided what might have otherwise turned into a humiliating experience.

NOTES

_____

_____

_____

_____

_____

_____

INTENTION VS. ATTENTION EXERCISES

1) List 3 examples of a situation in which you set your intention, or AIM, and through allowing your attention to be distracted completely missed the target.

2) List 3 examples of a situation in which you set your intention, or AIM, and through keeping your attention focused completely hit the target.

NOTES

_____

_____

_____

_____

_____

_____

_____

_____

_____

_____

_____

NEUTRALIZING RESISTING FORCE EXERCISES

1) List 3 examples of a situation in which you performed an action against your better judgment, that resulted in feelings of regret, guilt, and/or embarrassment. Did you try to stop yourself, but couldn't? What could you have done differently?

2) List 3 examples of a situation in which you could not perform an action that would have benefited you and possibly others, regardless of how hard you tried, because there was overwhelming opposition from either within or without. What held you back? What could you have done differently?

3) List 3 examples of a situation in which you felt stuck and/or helpless, and immediately upon laughing aloud at yourself and the situation, a solution presented itself, freeing you to move forward. Try it some time. Laughter is powerful!

NOTES

Vibration & Velocity
Exercises

1) List 3 negative words or phrases you have used repeatedly that have manifested in synonymous ways in your life. Are you still using those words or phrases? Can you become more aware of the words or phrases you use in the future?

2) List 3 positive words or phrases you have used repeatedly that have manifested in synonymous ways in your life. Can you make a list of some of those words or phrases and incorporate them more often into your daily communications?

3) List 3 examples of a situation in which you were in such a hurry you completely mucked up what you were trying to accomplish. How would slowing down have changed the outcome? What else could you have done differently?

4) List 3 examples of a situation in which you were tempted to rush through or into something, but opted to take it slowly and, as a result, were successful in what you were trying to accomplish and/or averted a disaster.

NOTES

SMALL WORLD
EXERCISES

1) List 3 examples of a situation in which some-one helpful showed up spontaneously at just the right moment to assist. Were you "in tune" in that moment? Or, did the miracle "tune you in?" Did you express your gratitude internally as well as externally?

2) List 3 examples of a situation in which some-one you thought you had nothing in common with turned out to be a good friend. Did you learn that you actually had some thing(s) in common, after all?

NOTES

———————————————————

———————————————————

———————————————————

———————————————————

———————————————————

———————————————————

———————————————————

———————————————————

Surf the Wave
Exercises

1) List 3 examples of Full Moon lunacy you have partaken in during your lifetime.

2) List 3 examples of Full Moon fulfillment you have experienced during your lifetime.

NOTES

_____

_____

_____

_____

_____

_____

_____

_____

_____

_____

_____

_____

_____

SELF CARE
EXERCISE

Make a checklist to monitor your self-care regimen. Have this checklist visible and handy. Use it every day—a white board is useful since the check marks can be refreshed daily. Are you nurturing and nourishing yourself every day? What events cause you to skip meals, vitamins, exercise, playtime, meditation time? Isn't it time to start treating yourself with the love and respect that you deserve? Today is the first day of the rest of your life. Use it wisely...

Know Thyself!

Be your own best friend!!!

Acknowledgments

Writing this book has been much like my life—a labor of love. I find I am overwhelmed with gratitude for my mother for her steadfast support and unwavering faith that I would survive my tenuous teens and twenties to, eventually, come to my senses. My children's father who passed into the great beyond when our little ones were still in diapers, for driving the last nail through my ego's attachment to self-deception while he was still incarnate, and becoming my bridge to the infinite sea of multi-dimensional reality when he left this 3D environment. My sons who I cherish with all my heart, for loving me the best they could through my dis-ease and my healing. My bright and forthright oldest, for being my "devil's advocate," challenging me to manage my fiery emotions and think in new ways about life, the universe, and everything. My brilliant and sensitive youngest for comforting me in sad moments and making sure I would never be lonely by bringing me a number of stray cats and, finally, his own baby boy that he entrusted to my care when he and his spouse felt they could no longer be the healthiest parents. My beautiful, wonderful grandson-spiritson for filling my life with more joy and encouragement than I ever could have imagined and reading every new re-write of this book aloud to me so I could hear what I was trying to say. My loving husband of eleven years, who had a dream one night and ended up marrying this whole package; for shining his ever-present light through blue skies and stormy weather, and for his unending faith, hope, love, and patience as we continue to grow along spiritual lines. My heartfelt thank you to each of these souls, and to every other mentor and teacher, incarnate and otherwise, that my Higher Power has blessed me with along this journey. And, of course ... Sandy!

I love you all!

Pay it Forward

Gift a copy of this Letter-Book to a friend!
www.TheSweeteLife.com

About the Author

Jennifer Sweete is a Certified Massage Therapist and Holy Fire Karuna Reiki® Master and teacher, a Colorado small business consultant, musician, poet, writer and author of books and periodicals. Her written works have appeared in a variety of publications worldwide, and her music productions are available on CD and electronically. She is presently serving as President of the Writer's Exchange while working on her next book and loving her dedicated husband, high-tech teenage spiritson, and lazy cat.

Visit her website at www.TheSweeteLife.com.

NOTES

NOTES